THE
DOMINO
EFFECT

Keep Tipping!

J. D. Walt

2:2

THE
DOMINO
EFFECT

Colossians

J. D. WALT

Unless otherwise indicated, Scripture quotations are taken from the Holy Bible, New International Version®, NIV® Copyright ©1973, 1978, 1984, 2011 by Biblica, Inc.® Used by permission. All rights reserved worldwide.

Scripture quotations marked ESV are taken from The Holy Bible, English Standard Version. ESV® Permanent Text Edition® (2016). Copyright © 2001 by Crossway Bibles, a publishing ministry of Good News Publishers.

Scripture quotations marked KJV are taken from the Holy Bible, King James Version (public domain).

Scripture quotations marked NRSV are taken from the New Revised Standard Version Bible, copyright © 1989 the Division of Christian Education of the National Council of the Churches of Christ in the United States of America. Used by permission. All rights reserved.

Scripture quotations marked NLT are taken from the Holy Bible, New Living Translation, copyright ©1996, 2004, 2007, 2013, 2015 by Tyndale House Foundation. Used by permission of Tyndale House Publishers, Inc., Carol Stream, Illinois 60188. All rights reserved.

Printed in the United States of America

Cover and page design by Strange Last Name
Page layout by PerfecType, Nashville, Tennessee

Walt, John David.
  The domino effect : Colossians / J.D. Walt. – Frankin, Tennessee : Seedbed Publishing, ©2018.

  pages ; cm. – (Seedbed daily text)

  ISBN 9781628245592 (paperback)
  ISBN 9781628245608 (Mobi)
  ISBN 9781628245615 (ePub)
  ISBN 9781628245622 (uPDF)

  1. Bible. Colossians -- Meditations. 2. Spiritual exercises.
  I. Title. II. Series.

BS2715.54.W34 2018   227/.706   2018932513

SEEDBED PUBLISHING
Franklin, Tennessee
seedbed.com

Contents

How the Daily Text Works

It seems obvious to say, but I write the Daily Text every day. I mostly write it the day before it is scheduled to release online.

Speaking of that, before we go further, I would like to cordially invite you to subscribe and receive the daily email. Visit dailytext.seedbed.com to get started. Check out the weekly fasting challenge while you are there, and also the very active Facebook group.

Eventually, the daily postings become part of a Daily Text discipleship resource. That's what you hold in your hands now.

It's not exactly a Bible study, though the Bible is both the source and subject. You will learn something about the Bible along the way: its history, context, original languages, and authors. My goal is not educational in nature but transformational. I am more interested in our knowing Jesus than I am in our knowing *about* Jesus.

To that end, each reading begins with the definitive inspiration of the Holy Spirit, the ongoing, unfolding text of Scripture. Following this is a short and, hopefully, substantive insight from the text and some aspect of its meaning. For insight to lead to deeper influence, we turn the text into prayer. Finally, influence must run its course toward impact. This is why we ask each other questions. These questions are not designed to elicit information but to crystallize intention. Discipleship always leads from inspiration to intention and from attention to action.

Using the Daily Text as a Discipleship Curricular Resource for Groups

While Scripture always addresses us personally, it is not written to us individually. The content of Scripture cries out for a community to address. The Daily Text is made for discipleship in community. This resource can work in several different ways. It could be read like a traditional book, a few pages or chapters at a time. Though unadvisable, the readings could be crammed in on the night before the meeting. Keep in mind, the Daily Text is not called the *Daily* Text for kicks. We believe Scripture is worthy of our most focused and consistent attention. Every day. We all have misses, but let's make every day more than a noble aspiration. Let's make it our covenant with one another.

For Use with Bands

In our judgment, the best and highest use of the Daily Text is made through what we call *banded discipleship*. A band is a same-gender group of three to five people who read together, pray together, and meet together to help one another grow into the fullness of Jesus Christ in this life. With banded discipleship, the daily readings serve more as a common text for the band and grist for the interpersonal conversation mill between meetings. The band meeting is reserved for the specialized activities of high-bar discipleship.

To learn more about bands and banded discipleship, visit newroombands.com. Be sure to download the free *Guide to Micro-Community Discipleship* or order a supply of the printed booklets online. Also be sure to explore our online platform for bands at app.newroombands.com.

For Use with Classes and Small Groups

The Daily Text has also proven to be a helpful discipleship resource for a variety of small groups, from community groups to Sunday school classes. Here are some suggested guidelines for deploying the Daily Text as a resource for a small group or class setting.

I. Hearing the Text

Invite the group to settle into silence for a period of no less than one and no more than five minutes. Ask an appointed person to keep time and to read the biblical text covering the period of days since the last group meeting. Allow at least one minute of silence following the reading of the text.

II. Responding to the Text

Invite anyone from the group to respond to the reading by answering these prompts: What did you hear? What did you see? What did you otherwise sense from the Lord?

III. Sharing Insights and Implications for Discipleship

Moving in an orderly rotation (or free-for-all), invite people to share insights and implications from the week's readings. What did you find challenging, encouraging, provocative, comforting, invasive, inspiring, corrective, affirming, guiding, or warning? Allow group conversation to proceed at will. Limit to one sharing item per turn, with multiple rounds of discussion.

Note: this resource comes with a free series of online streaming videos for each week's group meeting. In them, I share a seven- to ten-minute reflection on some aspect of the Scripture readings from the prior week. Some groups like to play the video at the beginning of this group sharing time as a way of kicking off the conversation.

IV. Shaping Intentions for Prayer

Invite each person in the group to share a single discipleship intention for the week ahead. It is helpful if the intention can also be framed as a question the group can use to check in from the prior week. At each person's turn, he or she is invited to share how their intention went during the previous week.

The class or group can open and close their meeting according to their established patterns.

Introduction

The Domino Effect: Finding the Tipping Points of Faith "In Christ"

Have you ever played with dominoes? No, I didn't ask if you have ever played dominoes. I want to know if you have ever stacked dominoes end over end and arranged them into some kind of circle or design in order to tip the first one and, hopefully, begin the chain reaction of the next one falling and the next and the next.

I decided to google the practice. As of this writing, the Guinness world record for domino tipping is 15,524 dominoes. But I kept googling, only to find another Guinness record-setting feat of the largest number of dominoes to tip in a spiral arrangement. It came to 250,000. It took days to set the whole thing up and only minutes for them to tip and fall. It is quite an effect to see such a spectacle, but honestly, in no time it gets rather boring. It's predictable and leaves one ready to move on to googling Tannerite explosions and other online time sucks.

For too many of us and for too long, the Bible has been like a boneyard of flat dominoes. We have done our best to play around with them, but they have never come into alignment with the powerful effects of the Holy Spirit. Nor have our lives come into the alignment Jesus intends for the supernatural entity he referred to as "my church" (Matt. 16:18). I fear that the present-day church, which is a reflection of present-day Christians, has become something of an exercise in domino tipping. Enormous amounts of time are spent arranging our programs, classes, and events—just as we did them last year—and the dominoes tip and fall predictably and in order, like clockwork. We expect them to impress us and others, and they do for a little while, but if we are honest, we must admit to being a little bored with it all. Surely this is not what Jesus envisioned when he spoke of building his church on the rock and the gates of hell not prevailing against it (Matt. 16:18).

There are domino-tipping exercises that exhibit what is commonly referred to as "the domino effect," and then there's something altogether different that I consider to be the *real* domino effect. I'm talking about the way a two-inch-tall domino can tip into and topple over a four-and-a-half-inch-tall domino and the way a four-and-a-half-inch-tall domino can topple a domino just over a foot tall, and that one can fell a domino two-and-a-half-feet tall. Here's the power of the domino effect: when you get to the twenty-third domino in this progression, you've just toppled the Eiffel Tower. When you come to the thirty-first domino, you've just knocked over something three thousand feet higher than Mount Everest. Sit down for this next one. At domino number fifty-seven, you are approaching the moon! (I am indebted to Gary Keller, who first pointed me to the domino effect in his book *The One Thing: The Surprisingly Simple Truth Behind Extraordinary Results*.)

Some years ago, I became fixated on Colossians 2:2–3:

> My goal is that they may be encouraged in heart and united in love, so that they may have the full riches of complete understanding, in order that they may know the mystery of God, namely, Christ, in whom are hidden all the treasures of wisdom and knowledge.

It's not every day that we see one of the authors of Scripture make reference to "my goal." It caused me to lean forward and take note. Paul knew that if he could band people together in communities of love and encouragement, the gospel message would tip from information to transformation. He knew it would tip from being a message to revealing a mystery to becoming a movement.

The epiphany hit me like a box of dominoes. For me, Colossians 2:2 would henceforth and forever be known as Domino #2|2, and I was off to the store to purchase a box set. I actually bought a lot of sets, and from each one I carefully searched for and removed the 2|2 domino. I wanted one for each member of our team.

As I worked my way through Paul's letter to the Colossians, the subject of this book, the domino epiphany hit me again. I began to see dominoes all over the place. There's Domino #1|2, the "In Christ," "in Colossae" Domino (1:2). Then there's Domino #1|9, which says, "For this reason, since the day we heard about you, we have not stopped praying for you. We continually ask God to fill you with the knowledge of his will through all the wisdom and understanding that the Spirit gives" (1:9). Then there's Domino #1|13, The 9-1-1 Domino. After that comes Domino #1|27, The Secret. Those three little words Paul referred to as "the secret" (1:27 NLT), which are "Christ in you" (1:27 ESV), just may be the most powerful tipping point of them all.

Each of these dominoes holds enormous capacity to topple things far exceeding their size, and when arranged together, they hold the ever-present potential to tip fresh movements of awakening. We all know and remember when the dominoes started tipping in our own lives and faith. Imagine that unleashed in the world. That's exactly what happened from the moment Jesus began calling disciples to follow him. One life tipped into another life, which tipped into a family, which tipped into a village and a town and a countryside and a region.

Didn't Jesus describe to a tee the domino effect when he said to his disciples, "But you will receive power when the Holy Spirit comes on you; and you will be my witnesses in Jerusalem, and in all Judea and Samaria, and to the ends of the earth" (Acts 1:8)?

The dominoes tipped from the Upper Room with 120 people to the day of Pentecost with 3,000 and all the way to the present day and some 2 billion Christians around the world. In domino-effect terms we've been to the moon and back a thousand times and the dominoes are still falling.

Impossible things keep happening and great awakenings are still on the horizon.

What if we thought of these ancient verses as so many dominoes we could stand up end over end in our own lives, and what if we could so order and arrange our lives together that we might become a kind of domino effect in our church and our town and away to the ends of the earth? What if we learned to shoot for the moon?

That's the point of this journey through Colossians. We won't force anything; rather, we will playfully stand these texts end over end and invite them to tip our faith to the next level.

That's where we are headed—*The Domino Effect: Finding the Tipping Points of Faith "In Christ."* Who wants to tip first?

THE
DOMINO
EFFECT

Are You in the Picture or Are You the Frame?

COLOSSIANS 1:1–2 NRSV | Paul, an apostle of Christ Jesus by the will of God, and Timothy our brother, To the saints and faithful brothers and sisters in Christ in Colossae: Grace to you and peace from God our Father.

Consider This

Four words from the second verse will offer both picture and frame for this whole project of Paul's letter to the Colossians. Did you catch them?

in Christ
in Colossae

The big question: Which will be the picture and which will be the frame? Will this Roman city, with its culture and value system, dominate the picture, inviting the Christians and their church to provide a bit of baptismal window dressing for the big show? Or will the in-Christ-ones (i.e., Christians) supply the art, with the cultural context of "in Colossae" serving as the frame? Will those who are "in Christ" really live as if they are "in Christ," or will they choose to live more like those "in Colossae," blending in to the ever-turning and twisting cultural landscape as a kaleidoscopic chameleon might do?

In every age, from the first century to the twenty-first, there are always two primary alternatives: Will "in Christ" be dominant or will "in Colossae"? There is the prevailing religious system and then there is real Christianity. It's practical, conventional, and insanely reasonable. The prevailing religious system mimics the real thing at many points, with its hat tips to God, public invocations, and Judeo-Christian–based social customs, offering a palatable civic religion most patrons will readily salute.

The issue is not whether we will live in Colossae or not. We must live there or in Cincinnati, or Centerville, or wherever it is we have been appointed to live. The question is whether we will live *in Christ* or not. Will I become a bona fide in-Christ-one? This is the awakening we must have. This begins to happen when our attention turns from our disgruntlement with the insanity around us to our discontent with the incongruity within us. When this awakening becomes greater and greater within us, it leads to the awakening becoming greater and greater around us.

That's Domino #1|2: In Christ in Colossae.

The Prayer

Abba Father, we thank you for your Son, Jesus, who would give himself to us so completely that we would become unmistakably like him. Turn my attention from what is wrong with the world to what is wrong in my own life. Come, Holy Spirit, and stir me to a deeper awakening.

I want to be "in Christ," a real Christian. We pray in Jesus' name. Amen.

The Questions

- What do you make of this picture-and-frame analogy with respect to "in Christ" and "in Colossae"?
- Are you tired of the conventional religion of cultural Christianity? What ways do you see that "in America" (or your own context) has corrupted what it means to live "in Christ"?
- What will it look like to turn the focus from the problems out there onto your own life and faith?

On the Difference between Knowledge and Knowing

2

COLOSSIANS 1:3–6 NRSV | In our prayers for you we always thank God, the Father of our Lord Jesus Christ, for we have heard of your faith in Christ Jesus and of the love that you have for all the saints, because of the hope laid up for you in heaven. You have heard of this hope before in the word of the truth, the gospel that has come to you. Just as it is bearing fruit and growing in the whole world, so it has been bearing fruit among yourselves from the day you heard it and truly comprehended the grace of God.

Consider This

The thing that stands in the way of my truly comprehending God's grace is that I'm pretty sure I already truly comprehend it. Go back and read that sentence again.

While the gospel is a message, it cannot be confined to messages. While the gospel is the truth, it cannot be captured by a series of propositional truths. Before the gospel is anything else, the gospel is God. *Gospel* means "good news," and the good news is God. The good news is not that God loves us. It is that God is love. The good news is not that Jesus saves. It is that Jesus is himself salvation.

We think we truly comprehend God and the gospel because we have some comprehension of what God has done for us. This is good, as far as it goes, but it does not go anywhere near far enough. When our understanding of the gospel is limited to what God has done for us, our understanding of sharing the gospel will be limited to telling others what God has done for them.

To be sure, the gospel is the message of what God has done for us in Jesus Christ, but in a far greater sense, the gospel is who Jesus Christ is to us and in us and through us for the world. The gospel is not a body of knowledge about who God is and what God has done. It is actually *knowing* God. Jesus prayed, "Now this is eternal life: that they know you, the only true God, and Jesus Christ, whom you have sent" (John 17:3).

We have lived through a period of world history wherein the measure of mastery consisted in knowing about a subject. The Christian faith is not meant for this paradigm. Real Christianity can never be reduced to knowing about God. We must go on to knowing God. To think one can master the subject of God is the ultimate idolatry. Real Christianity is about understanding oneself as subject to God and becoming mastered by Jesus Christ.

The gospel of Jesus Christ is not God's solution to our sin problem. The gospel is that "God was reconciling the world to himself in Christ, not counting [our] sins against [us]" (2 Cor. 5:19). It is a reconciled relationship through which God lives in us and we in him. The gospel is not the knowledge but the knowing. The domain of knowledge is in a body of information. The domain of knowing is in the body of Jesus Christ. And none of this is meant to eschew or despise knowledge, but rather to say that knowledge is a penultimate understanding. Ultimate comprehension means knowledge about God must give way to knowing God.

> Just as it is bearing fruit and growing in the whole world, so it has been bearing fruit among yourselves from the day you heard it and truly comprehended the grace of God. (Col. 1:6 NRSV)

To become a real "in Christ" Christian is our aim. Most often, it requires us to humble ourselves and confess that we might not be there quite yet; not that we aren't on the way, but that the Way just might be a whole lot more than we ever comprehended.

Domino #1|6, let's call it The Comprehension Test.

The Prayer

Abba Father, we thank you for your Son, Jesus, who is both the Way and the way maker. He is the life and the life giver. He is the truth, not as a construct of knowledge but as a person, the Word made flesh. I want to know Jesus more than I want to know *about* him. I want to know him personally and intimately and powerfully. To this end we pray in Jesus' name. Amen.

The Questions

- Does your knowledge about God outstrip your knowing of God? Will you allow this to rise to the level of a holy discontent within you?
- Are you ready to invite the Holy Spirit to lead you to the next place of knowing Jesus? What will this look like?
- Does your pride in your knowledge about God hold you back from the kind of humility required to know God more?

Why I Can't Be a Professional Anymore

3

COLOSSIANS 1:7–10 | You learned it from Epaphras, our dear fellow servant, who is a faithful minister of Christ on our behalf, and who also told us of your love in the Spirit. For this reason, since the day we heard about you, we have not stopped praying for you. We continually ask God to fill you with the knowledge of his will through all the wisdom and understanding that the Spirit gives, so that you may live a life worthy of the Lord and please him in every way: bearing fruit in every good work, growing in the knowledge of God.

Consider This

As is often the case, I am convicted by today's text, but in a way that may surprise you. It's not about being filled with the knowledge of God's will and wisdom and understanding and living a life worthy of the Lord and pleasing the Lord in every way and bearing fruit in every good work and all that. Don't get me wrong; this is the stuff of conviction, but that's not it today. Two phrases tackled me today:

We have not stopped praying
We continually ask God

These early Christians took prayer seriously. My friend David Thomas regularly reminds us in our work with the

New Room that the Bible is "utterly unfamiliar with casual prayer." How is it that I can be so casual when it comes to prayer? I was asked recently to lead a couple of prayer conferences, which has brought me to a place of conviction about my own prayer life.

It has me remembering the early days of my own awakening, when I prayed all the time. In those days I could have fairly identified with Paul's words, "we have not stopped praying," and "we continually ask God." There were very regular set times of prayer. There was spontaneous prayer throughout the day. I prayed with other people all the time. I prayed alone, even through the night at times. It wasn't duty but delight. I loved to talk with God and to be in agreement with others in their prayers before God. I'd love to tell you some stories sometime.

If you have read the Daily Text for any length of time, you know I try to keep it real. If I'm keeping it real, I must tell you that I may be more committed to the idea of prayer than I am to prayer itself. I believe in it. I'm for it. I'm just not praying very much these days. Sometimes I think I try to convince myself that I am so spiritually mature that I am really praying all the time; that somehow my thoughts are my prayers; or that I have moved beyond defined times and set prayers. I'm just going to call it today.

I want to get back to the place where I can say with loving authenticity things like, "I have not stopped praying," and "I continually ask God . . ."

Here's where I think I went wrong. Somewhere along the way, I turned pro. What I once did for the love of the game, I began doing as a job. And I think that's OK to a point, but when it comes to prayer, there's no such thing as a professional. We are all amateurs. Now, there's a word I think I have misunderstood. I have thought of an amateur as someone who doesn't really take the game seriously. The term gets used pejoratively so often, as in, "He's such an amateur." It means something altogether different. Amateur comes from the Latin word *amare*, which means "to love." An amateur plays, or in this case prays, for the love of it.

There it is. Nine verses into the first round and Colossians takes me to the mat. I'm not ready to tap out, but I am surrendering my professional prayer credentials today. I'm returning to amateur status. That's how you can pray for me.

Anybody out there with me?

Turning Amateur—that's what I'm calling Domino #1|9. When this one tips, big obstacles start falling.

The Prayer

Abba Father, we thank you for your Son, Jesus, who both teaches us to pray and answers our prayers. Come, Holy Spirit, and fill me with the tenacious faith of Jesus in my praying. Bring fresh definition to my prayer life, new dimension and an awakened sensitivity to your presence. Lord, teach me to pray anew. We pray in Jesus' name. Amen.

The Questions

- How about you? Do "we have not stopped praying" and "we continually ask God" describe your prayer life at this time?
- What do you make of this professional-versus-amateur contrast? Have you made the ill-fated move to turn professional in your prayer life before?
- In what particular ways do you feel burdened or called to grow in your life of prayer?

4 That Time I Had to Be Rescued

COLOSSIANS 1:11–14 NRSV | May you be made strong with all the strength that comes from his glorious power, and may you be prepared to endure everything with patience, while joyfully giving thanks to the Father, who has enabled you to share in the inheritance of the saints in the light. He has rescued us from the power of darkness and transferred us into the kingdom of his beloved Son, in whom we have redemption, the forgiveness of sins.

Consider This

Things may not always be as black and white as we want them to be, but of this we can be sure: there is a kingdom of light and a dominion of darkness. Unfortunately, we are all born into the dominion of darkness. This is the only plausible explanation for the unbridled desecration of creation and the enormity of brokenness in the world.

The gospel is that we have a God who "has enabled [us] to share in the inheritance of the saints in the light" (Col. 1:12 NRSV). This is how God did it: "He has rescued us from the power of darkness and transferred us into the kingdom of his beloved Son, in whom we have redemption, the forgiveness of sins" (Col. 1:13–14 NRSV).

We must be rescued. Until we realize this we will remain lost.

I will never forget the time I had to be rescued. I was fifteen and deer hunting after school in an expansive tract of woods near our farm. At dusk, I spotted a buck, took aim, and felled the deer; or so I thought. He ran for what seemed like miles. After a solid hour of tracking, I found him, only to realize I was lost. And did I mention it was dark? I cried out in desperation for help. I fired my rifle down to the last shell. I could sense hordes of predators just out of sight, creeping toward me to devour my prey (and me!). No one came. They didn't even know I was there. I was caught in the literal dominion of darkness. I could not see my hand in front of my face.

I needed to be rescued. I was, proverbially speaking, "deep in the heart of Texas" (only it was Arkansas). I would not find my way out of this fix, not even in the light of day. Time moved like a dead snail, when finally, I saw what looked like a flickering light in the distance. Then I heard his voice shouting my name, "John David! John David!" It was my father. He had come to rescue me. With tears in my eyes, I ran toward that light and into the safety of his embrace.

That's what rescue looks like, literally and figuratively. You can do the math from here. You already have.

I think I used to think I didn't need to be rescued, that I wasn't one of those kinds of people. Sure, I knew I was a sinner, but not that bad. I just needed a little Sunday school–esque straightening of the collar. Now I know better. The kind of sinner I thought I was is actually the worst kind of sinner because we think that since we didn't ride the *Titanic* to the bottom of the ocean, we somehow don't need as much grace as the ones who did. Now I recognize this as a lie from the pit of hell. The dominion of darkness is oh-so-deceptive. We all must be rescued, especially me. In fact, I will never become a real Christian until I know I am a real sinner.

Let us henceforth refer to Domino #1|13 as The 9-1-1 Domino.

The Prayer

Abba Father, we thank you for your Son, Jesus, who came into the deep, dark woods of this world, light in hand, to find us. We didn't mean to get lost, but we did. Let me never forget the story of your rescuing me, lest I wander away again. And make me an agent of your rescue for others. We pray in Jesus' name. Amen.

The Questions

- Do you know your rescue story?
- How can we help one another to live fully in the kingdom of light?
- Have you learned to spot the creeping shadows of the dominion of darkness? What does it look like in your life? How are you learning to run toward the light?

Did You Know You Are a Worship Leader?

5

COLOSSIANS 1:15–18 | The Son is the image of the invisible God, the firstborn over all creation. For in him all things were created: things in heaven and on earth, visible and invisible, whether thrones or powers or rulers or authorities; all things have been created through him and for him. He is before all things, and in him all things hold together. And he is the head of the body, the church; he is the beginning and the firstborn from among the dead, so that in everything he might have the supremacy.

Consider This

I am a worship leader. No, I don't play guitar and lead songs, but I am a worship leader. You are too. It's our highest calling and one that will never end. Our lives will be defined by our worship, and our worship will, for better or worse, lead the worship of others.

Some of you don't know that I work for a seminary. Seedbed is a mission of Asbury Theological Seminary. Before I got involved with Seedbed, I served eleven years as the dean of the chapel on our Kentucky campus, which means I served as a pastor to hundreds of men and women preparing to serve the church.

A major part of the job involved designing and leading corporate worship for three different gatherings throughout the week—coming to about a thousand gatherings before we were done. Our main objective was to lift up as beautiful and big and bold a vision of Jesus as possible every single time. The inside joke was we approached Jesus in worship like we approached voting in Arkansas in the old days—early and often. How soon could we begin talking about Jesus? How quickly could we say his name? What stories could we tell about him? Every time he gets lifted up, he draws people to him.

Here we are, only fifteen verses in, and Paul is casting an utterly stratospheric vision of the Son of God. He does this in all his letters: Jesus early and Jesus often. Check out the first few lines of it again:

> The Son is the image of the invisible God, the firstborn over all creation. For in him all things were created: things in heaven and on earth, visible and invisible, whether thrones or powers or rulers or authorities; all things have

been created through him and for him. He is before all things, and in him all things hold together. (vv. 15–17)

We must see Jesus. We were made to behold him. His life, not in general but in a thousand specific ways, must become our vision. His preexistence, preeminence, conception, birth, life, words, deeds, miracles, relationships, signs, sermons, parables, prayers, suffering, passion, death, burial, resurrection, ascension, return, and eternal reign must become our holy obsession. This is the message Paul offers the Colossians and the Colombians, the Americans and the Africans, and everyone else. We must see Jesus. We must fix our gaze upon him.

Why is this so important? Because we become like what or whom we behold. We will behold someone or something. That we will worship is a given. Whom or what we will worship is up for grabs. Because we are made in the image of God, and because Jesus is the image of God, and because we will not find our true selves until we find ourselves in him, we must see Jesus.

As his life becomes the source and substance of our lives, we become the people God imagined when he first imagined us. As we become those particular people, our lives (and, particularly, our relationships) lead his worship and others see the vision.

Like it or not, we are worship leaders, you and me. Where are we leading those we seek to lead?

You are getting the hang of this. So, what will you call Domino #1|15?

The Prayer

Abba Father, we thank you for your Son, Jesus, who leads us all in triumphal procession. He is the image of the invisible God; the firstborn over all creation; the Lamb of God, who takes away the sins of the world; the Alpha and Omega; the One who holds all things together, in whom we live and move and have our being. Open the eyes of our hearts to see him in all his lowliness and in all his exaltedness. We must see Jesus. We pray in Jesus' name. Amen.

The Questions

- How does today's daily text both challenge and encourage you?
- How will you "turn your eyes upon Jesus," as the 1920s hymn encourages us to do? How will Jesus more and more become your vision?
- What does a daily habit and practice of beholding Jesus look like for you? How can that grow? You will only grow as this grows.

Is God Really a Human Being?

6

COLOSSIANS 1:19–20 | For God was pleased to have all his fullness dwell in him, and through him to reconcile to himself all things, whether things on earth or things in heaven, by making peace through his blood, shed on the cross.

Consider This

As we begin with today's text, I want to ask you to stop and slowly say aloud the twelve words that compose Colossians 1:19:

For God was pleased to have all his fullness dwell in him.

If you are listening, press pause and say those words aloud and slowly.

It's one of the recurring themes on the Daily Text, but Paul wants us to be clear: yes, Jesus is God, but even more so, God is Jesus!

Does it strike you as a bit of a redundancy to say, "all his fullness"? Does not the word "fullness" imply "all"? What's going on here? The Greek word is pronounced "play-ro-mah." It means something like perfect completion on the one hand, and on the other, superabundance. It carries both the ideas of quality of fullness and quantity of fullness. Every bit of the God of the universe, both in terms of the qualities of God and the sheer quantity of God, lives in Jesus Christ. Paul wants us to grasp the ungraspable. It's as if he's saying, "extra-complete." Because it would seem impossible for God to be contained in a human being, Paul is inspired to make the point even stronger.

In Jesus, we see just what kind of human being God actually is. Wow! That is a stretcher of a sentence right there. God is a human being. We don't struggle so much with God as a divine being, but when it comes down to it, we struggle with God as a human being. Something deep in all of us wants to escape being human. We want to be superhuman (hence our fascination with superheroes). What we want, though we wouldn't admit it, is to be gods. We want to be in control, to be the masters of our own destiny and the destiny of others. We don't want to be more and greater and better; we want to be the most and the greatest and the best. We want to be sovereign.

As a point of theology, herein lies the problem of seeing God primarily through a lens of sovereignty. In our brokenness and depravity, we do not understand sovereignty. We see it as power and control. We must see sovereignty as God sees sovereignty, which is not the power of control but the power of love. It is also true to say in our brokenness and depravity that we do not understand love. This is why we must see Jesus. We see God's sovereignty perfectly and completely when we see Jesus, because in Jesus we see the nature of true sovereignty as holy love. Jesus reveals to us and would restore in us the sovereignty we were meant to have as human beings, which is of the same nature as the sovereignty of God—not the power of dictatorial control but the power of divine, holy love. Verse 20 gives us the nature of God's sovereignty:

> and through him to reconcile to himself all things, whether things on earth or things in heaven, by making peace through his blood, shed on the cross.

God comes to us, who, in our sin, scrambled to take his place. Instead God, who knew no sin, became sin and took our place. As we forsook ourselves in order to become like God, God forsook himself to become like us. In fact, Tertullian, one of the great fathers of the church, said it something like this: "God became like us, so we could become like him."

For you see, if all the fullness of God dwells in Jesus Christ, this necessarily opens up the possibility that all the fullness of God can dwell in you and in me—more precisely, in us. This is the awakening we must have. We must abandon our slavish quest for godlike control and accept our gifted destiny as the recipients of God-like fullness.

If you don't believe me, stay tuned. And it's probably a good idea to buckle your seat belts if you haven't already.

That's Domino #1|19: Human-God.

The Prayer

Abba Father, we thank you for your Son, Jesus, in whom all of your fullness dwells. We thank you that Jesus is fully and completely God, that God is Jesus. And we thank you that Jesus is fully and completely human, that God is human.

J. D. WALT

Come, Holy Spirit, and cause us to grapple deeply with these eternal and yet earthly verities. We confess we cannot grasp it. Open the eyes of our hearts. We pray in Jesus' name. Amen.

The Questions

- Do you really believe that God is a human being? How do you struggle with this?
- Do you believe that as Jesus is, so we are meant to become? Again, where do you struggle with this?
- Talk about your own battle between the quest for godlike sovereignty and the aspiration for God-like love.

7 Can Jesus Be My Savior and Not Be My Lord?

COLOSSIANS 1:21–23 | Once you were alienated from God and were enemies in your minds because of your evil behavior. But now he has reconciled you by Christ's physical body through death to present you holy in his sight, without blemish and free from accusation—if you continue in your faith, established and firm, and do not move from the hope held out in the gospel. This is the gospel that you heard and that has been proclaimed to every creature under heaven, and of which I, Paul, have become a servant.

Consider This

We have lived through a period of history in which the gospel has been presented with two options: the basic package and the deluxe package. The basic package would include Jesus Christ as Savior. The deluxe package includes Jesus Christ as Lord. In other words, one can check the box for Jesus Christ as Savior and not go for the upgrade with Jesus as Lord. Through another lens, the Jesus Christ as Savior package was like a fire insurance policy. The Jesus Christ as Lord package was more like a complete home renovation project.

What do you think most people bought? Yep, the insurance policy. Jesus can be my Savior, and maybe I will get around to making him my Lord someday. I hate to be the bearer of bad news, but this is not the good news. The gospel makes one offer. I like the way missionary E. Stanley Jones put it: "Jesus Christ will be Lord of all or he will not be Lord at all."

So, what does all of this have to do with today's text? Did you notice the big, fat, two-letter word right in the middle of the Scripture today? Yes, it's "if."

The big if of real Christianity is this one: "if you continue in your faith, established and firm, and do not move from the hope held out in the gospel" (v. 23a).

With every good "if" comes a "then," so what is the then?

> But now he has reconciled you by Christ's physical body through death to present you holy in his sight, without blemish and free from accusation. (v. 22)

What's going on here? How is something that seems to have unequivocally happened in the past—and doesn't even contain the word *then*—now conditioned by something that must keep happening in the future? Is our salvation dependent on our own persistence? No, Scripture makes abundantly clear that "it is by grace you have been saved, through faith—and this is not from yourselves, it is the gift of God" (Eph. 2:8).

The issue is not God's grace. It is our faith. Colossians 1:22 is all grace:

> But now he has reconciled you by Christ's physical body through death to present you holy in his sight, without blemish and free from accusation.

Colossians 1:23 is all faith:

> if you continue in your faith, established and firm, and do not move from the hope held out in the gospel.

The gospel is forensic in its nature, with a definite transactional sense. God canceled the debt, reconciling us to God. However, the gospel is relational in its character and essence. The sign of grace from God is the immovable cross. The sign of faith from us is the movemental cross. Because God has moved once and for all in Jesus Christ, we can move now and forevermore through Jesus Christ. The sign that we have been moved by grace is that we are moving in faith. People for whom Jesus is Lord are necessarily living and moving in faith.

If a person is not moving in faith, chances are he or she is/was not moved by grace but by something else. Real Christianity demands that we become brutally honest with ourselves and one another about matters of such gravity.

So, am I saying that many people who claim to be Christians may not be real Christians? I'm saying the real question is the one we must ask ourselves: Am I a real Christian?

So, can Jesus be one's Savior and not one's Lord? For what it's worth, I say no—not and still be a real Christian.

Nothing tips until one surrenders to Jesus as Lord. Until then one just stands there. Domino #1|23 is a super tipping point.

The Prayer

Abba Father, we thank you for your Son, Jesus, who is himself the embodiment of grace and the activity of faith. Teach me that yesterday's faith is like yesterday's manna— enough for yesterday. Lead me to the faith of today, to stretch and grow and reach for more of you. We pray in Jesus' name. Amen.

The Questions

- How do you sort out this big "then" and "if" in verses 22–23 of today's text?
- How do you relate to this notion of grace as the "immovable cross" and faith as the "movemental cross"?
- Is salvation for you more of a past transaction or a present and ongoing movement? How can we help others with this distinction?

The Problem with St. Francis's Most Famous Quote That He Never Really Said

8

COLOSSIANS 1:24 NRSV | I am now rejoicing in my sufferings for your sake, and in my flesh I am completing what is lacking in Christ's afflictions for the sake of his body, that is, the church.

Consider This

Somewhere along the way we got the impression that sharing the gospel with another person meant telling him or her the plan of salvation. You know what I'm talking about—telling another person the four spiritual laws or the Roman Road or drawing the famous "Bridge to Life" diagram or some other approach. Paul gives us a profound image today of what sharing the gospel means and looks like:

> I am now rejoicing in my sufferings for your sake, and
> in my flesh I am completing what is lacking in Christ's
> afflictions for the sake of his body, that is, the church.
> (v. 24 NRSV)

While the gospel can never be less than recounting the story of Jesus Christ, it must be much more than this. The gospel moves on the muscles of love, and the muscles of love grow through acts of un-self-interested giving, a.k.a. suffering. By suffering, I don't mean a grit-your-teeth-and-bear-it kind of activity but a gladly-putting-others-first kind of activity. When suffering is done with love, it does not feel like suffering but like joy. Hence, Paul rejoices!

The gospel is complete in and of itself. It is the perfect offering of the love of God for us. Though it is complete, it must be extended, and it must be extended with the same character with which it was first given. I am becoming more and more convinced that we can tell people about Jesus all day long and still not extend the gospel. Why? Because the gospel is more than simply telling people about Jesus. It is more than an explanation about Jesus. It is a demonstration of Jesus. In fact, if you have to make a choice between telling someone about Jesus and showing him or her Jesus, you should probably do the latter. Why? Because someone may not remember what you said, but he or she will never forget what you did.

We've all heard the apocryphal quote often attributed to Saint Francis of Assisi, "Preach the gospel everywhere. If necessary use words." Can we be honest? People tend to like this because they would rather avoid the awkwardness of talking about Jesus. Permit me a moment of unvarnished keeping-it-real truth-telling. The nature and character of the gospel do not tend to come through the deeds of a person who does not want to talk about Jesus. (And because I know I will be hearing from my dad about my use of the term "apocryphal," I'll get out in front of that by saying *apocryphal* means Saint Francis didn't say it. For crying out loud, Saint Francis preached the gospel to animals—with words!)

In summary, sharing the gospel is a fully embodied act of ordinary yet supernatural love for other people. It involves our words, our deeds, our dispositions, and our overall posture and bearing toward other people. It means "I am completing what is lacking in Christ's afflictions for the sake of his body, that is, the church" (Col. 1:24b NRSV).

When we truly share the gospel, it always comes at a cost to ourselves, and yet it always makes us more than we were before. This is why the power of the gospel is found only in the way of the cross.

When we get involved with Jesus, he stretches our lives in the shape of the cross. It's why we are calling Domino #1|24 The Stretcher.

The Prayer

Abba Father, we thank you for your Son, Jesus, in whose whole life we see the whole cross; in whose love we see the mystery of suffering; and in whose suffering we see our calling to live a life of self-giving love for others. Bring this truth to reality in my life. Reveal to me what holds me back. We pray in Jesus' name. Amen.

The Questions

- What do you think of this assertion that we can tell people about Jesus all day long and not be sharing the gospel?

- What about the notion that we can do good things for people all day long and not be sharing the gospel?
- Are you uncomfortable with telling other people about Jesus? Why? What do you learn about yourself in this?

The Two Words That Changed Everything

9

COLOSSIANS 1:25–27 | I have become its servant by the commission God gave me to present to you the word of God in its fullness—the mystery that has been kept hidden for ages and generations, but is now disclosed to the Lord's people. To them God has chosen to make known among the Gentiles the glorious riches of this mystery, which is Christ in you, the hope of glory.

Consider This

What if I told you the prime difference between the New Testament and the Old Testament could be summarized in two words? You already know what they are, don't you?

In the Old Testament, the presence of God presented all around God's people. God was in the cloud by day and the pillar of fire by night. God resided between the cherubim on the mercy seat atop the ark of the covenant in the Most Holy Place deep in the heart of the tabernacle and later in the temple. God was with his people. At the same time there was this building prophecy that God would be Immanuel, God-with-us, even more so in the future, with the coming of Messiah.

Messiah did, in fact, come, in the person of Jesus of Nazareth, the God-Man. God was now with us in human flesh. Immanuel the promise, was now Immanuel the person. Still, the vision was not yet realized. Jesus told his disciples that unless and until he ascended to the Father, the Holy Spirit would not come.

The mystery, long hidden and now revealed, is not God with us. It is Christ in us. This was the vision from the start— the vision of Eden; not just God with us, but God in us.

We think so much of the presence of God as a kind of phenomenon that exists around us. The New Testament primarily envisages the presence of God as dwelling within us. We have thought so much about the plan of salvation as getting us into heaven. All along the plan of salvation has been to get heaven into us.

The two words that changed everything? *In you.*

Domino #1|27 shall henceforth be called The Secret.

The Prayer

Abba Father, we thank you for your Son, Jesus, who, more than with us, would dwell within us. Awaken me to this mystery and make it my reality: Christ in me. We pray in Jesus' name. Amen.

The Questions

- Do you think more of God being with you, or in you?
- What are the implications of Christ being in you?
- What would it mean and look like for you to become more attuned to the reality of Jesus Christ dwelling in you through the presence of the Holy Spirit?

Fully Mature?

10

COLOSSIANS 1:28–29 | He is the one we proclaim, admonishing and teaching everyone with all wisdom, so that we may present everyone fully mature in Christ. To this end I strenuously contend with all the energy Christ so powerfully works in me.

Consider This

For Paul the church was not an organization but a group of people. Therefore, growing the church, for Paul, was never about growing an organization but about growing people. He says it again so clearly in today's text:

> He is the one we proclaim, admonishing and teaching everyone with all wisdom, so that we may present everyone fully mature in Christ. (v. 28)

Paul's goal was not to get as many people as he possibly could to accept Christ. Sure, he wanted people to come to grips with their sin problem and to enter into a saving relationship with Jesus, but that was only the beginning. Paul's goal was to get as many people as he possibly could to the place of full maturity "in Christ." He did not have a starting-line mind-set but a finish-line mentality:

> . . . so that we may present everyone fully mature in Christ. (v. 1:28b)

So often these days, our approach centers around trying to get people to come to church, where we hope they will decide to keep coming back and, through the process, hear the gospel and become a Christian somewhere along the way. Sure, we want people to mature in their faith, and to that end we try to get them involved in all manner of church activity, much of it in the name of discipleship, but we have no way to know what's really happening along those lines, so in the meantime we do our best to take care of them and be there for them through life's ups and downs.

I don't mean this as a cynical criticism but as an honest observation. Most church leaders I know, lay and clergy, feel the same way. It's no one's fault. It is what it is at this point in the game. Tweaking the model will not get it done. We need a new model—really, we need an old way.

What if we approached the starting line with a finish-line mentality, "so that we may present everyone fully mature in Christ" (v. 28b)? How would that change the way we thought about life and faith and church?

Domino #1|28, though we call it Finish Line, must tip well before we get there if we hope to arrive.

The Prayer

Abba Father, we thank you for your Son, Jesus, who is our picture of what a mature human being looks like and who, through the person of the Holy Spirit, brings us to maturity in him. Awaken me to the ways I must mature, and fill me with your Spirit to this end. We pray in Jesus' name. Amen.

The Questions

- Describe in detail the picture of a mature follower of Jesus. What are the top three or four qualities?
- Who in your life and past strikes you as a mature Christian? What stands out to you about him or her?
- How might we find ways to measure maturity in an appropriate fashion? Everything we care about in life, we find ways to measure. How about this?

Christ in Y'all versus Christ in You

11

COLOSSIANS 2:1–3 | I want you to know how hard I am contending for you and for those at Laodicea, and for all who have not met me personally. My goal is that they may be encouraged in heart and united in love, so that they may have the full riches of complete understanding, in order that they may know the mystery of God, namely, Christ, in whom are hidden all the treasures of wisdom and knowledge.

Consider This

When we see a writer of Scripture use the two words "my goal," we should lean forward a bit because we are about to find gold. Of course, all Scripture is gold, but I think we can agree there are those extra 24-karat gold deposits.

Colossians 2:2–3 served as the focus of my work for more than a decade as I pastored the community of preparing pastors at Asbury Theological Seminary. For our team, this text served as the focus and force behind our work in creating a community that formed men and women into mature followers of Jesus Christ. We developed a shorthand, or symbol, among our team that we used in all manner of signs: 2:2. Yes, the whole domino effect idea began with #2|2.

Colossians 2:2 became "our goal" and the organizing principle of what a growing community of growing people should look like. Let's break down the passage and take a closer look.

1. "Know the mystery." Let's begin with the end in mind. As with all his churches, Paul wanted the Colossians to know something beyond what mere knowledge could convey to them. After all, a mystery is a mystery because it is unknowable in the conventional sense. Knowing a mystery is something of an oxymoron, isn't it?

2. "The mystery is Jesus Christ." More specifically, just a couple of verses back, Paul told us the mystery, long hidden and now revealed, is Christ in you (Col. 1:27). This is indeed a mystery, and Paul points it out because it is the proverbial gold mine of all gold mines: Christ, "in whom are hidden all the treasures of wisdom and knowledge" (2:3). The very meaning of life is hidden in this mystery: Christ in you. We can stop our quest for all the false treasure that isn't treasure because the true treasure, real wealth, unsurpassed riches, even, is now available to us.

3. The way is together. Here's the part that is not apparent to those of us who happen to be twenty-first-century Americans. When Paul identifies the mystery as "Christ in you," what he really means is "Christ in y'all." The *you*, as is the case so often in the New Testament, is plural. The New Testament rarely addresses me as an isolated, individuated, privatized person. To be sure, God addresses me personally, but my identity is not primarily as an individual. In fact, this is more a sign of my brokenness. I simply cannot know who I am outside of my relationship with God. And here's the kicker: I can't know God apart from other people. That's where we want to push back.

4. This explains Paul's goal: "My goal is that they may be encouraged in heart and united in love" (v. 2a). Paul understands his task as that of crafting courageous communities of profound love. Love is the means and the end, the way and the goal, the beginning and the end. The biblical idea of love has no meaning outside of relationship. For the gospel

to be the gospel, it requires a community of people, and even two or three will do. The gospel advances on the supernatural power of courageous love.

5. Note Paul's emphatic redundancy: not just riches, but "full riches," and not just "understanding" but "complete understanding." Paul is reaching for something that can hardly be expressed in words. He's trying to tell us there is something we are missing and will miss until we find one another "in Christ," which is to say together enjoying the fellowship of the Holy Spirit.

6. This is why banding together is so critical if we are going to sow for a great awakening. "Christ in you" only comes to full expression when it becomes "Christ in y'all," or as my more Southern colleagues point out, "Christ in all y'all!" This will not happen in our churches in any significant way until it begins to happen significantly in many small ways, that is, with a growing number of small bands of people who become "encouraged in heart and united in love."

OK, I'll just show you my cards. That's "my goal" for you— encouraged in heart and united in love . . . banded together to sow for a great awakening. And all this time you thought this was a daily devotion.

The Prayer

Abba Father, we thank you for your Son, Jesus, who with you and the Holy Spirit band together to show us the perfect picture of what encouraged in heart and united in love looks like. Band us together in the same way you are banded together, that you might awaken the world through our love. We pray in Jesus' name. Amen.

The Questions

- What do you think of the implications of "Christ in y'all" versus "Christ in you"?
- How will we overcome our deep formation as privatized individuals in order to express the gospel as God intends — through our relationships?
- Are you in a band, or do you need a band? Are you open to banding in the way I am talking about?

A Warning about My Fine-Sounding Arguments

12

COLOSSIANS 2:4–5 | I tell you this so that no one may deceive you by fine-sounding arguments. For though I am absent from you in body, I am present with you in spirit and delight to see how disciplined you are and how firm your faith in Christ is.

Consider This

It is not entirely clear what Paul is talking about in this letter to the Colossians, though he is clearly warning against false teaching. He is likely dealing with some form of Gnosticism, a heresy that didn't discard biblical teaching but distorted it in dangerous ways.

Then and now, the greatest danger to the gospel is not from outsiders or non-Christians, but from the insiders. Today's false teachers aren't the proponents of Scientology; rather, they are Christian leaders who attempt to set aside the clear teaching of Scripture in favor of something more palatable to modern hearers—a.k.a. fine-sounding arguments.

Fine-sounding arguments abound all over the place and from very respectable teachers. I read them all the time. For instance, I hear Fr. Richard Rohr regularly eschew what he calls a dualistic mind-set, or binary thinking, as though there were not good and evil, light and darkness, and virtue or vice. He makes fine-sounding arguments, and what he is saying is not entirely false, but it can be very misleading to a well-intentioned follower of Jesus. Another example would be Rev. Adam Hamilton and his "three buckets" approach to Scripture, and how certain teachings of Scripture can be disregarded because they are no longer applicable or were never reflective of the character of God in the first place. Again, he makes plausible and fine-sounding arguments about this, but they can be quite slippery and even deceptive.

Please understand, I am not questioning the faith of these teachers. I am certainly not leveling a personal attack against them. A person can be guilty of false teaching without falling into the full-on category of a false teacher. We must be generous in our posture toward others, and yet we must also be discriminating about what we accept and embrace as orthodox teaching. Am I suggesting we disregard teachers like these? Not necessarily. I read both Richard Rohr and Adam Hamilton and find a lot of what they have to say helpful and even illuminating at times; however, I sift everything.

Furthermore, I do not set myself up as an authority when it comes to teachers like these. They are undoubtedly more learned and experienced than I, yet I have a duty to call it as I see it and trust that others will do with that as they see fit.

Finally, just because I might raise questions about different teachers and teachings does not mean I place myself above them. In fact, I put myself in their same category: frail sinners and fallible human beings. I am fully aware of my skilled capacity to craft a fine-sounding argument that in the end may not pass muster. I fully expect my readers, be they advocates or detractors, to scripturally sift all I am saying and to invite the Holy Spirit to confirm it or call it into question. You who have been reading for any length of time know me by now and that I welcome feedback and pushback. It's one of the ways we love each other.

Be on your guard for Domino #2|4. Fine-sounding arguments that turn out to be wrong can tip the whole project in the wrong direction.

The Prayer

Abba Father, we thank you for your Son, Jesus, who is the truth, both in his words, and in his ways and his life. Grant me the gifts of a generous heart and a discerning mind when it comes to other people and their teaching. I want neither to mislead nor to be misled. I want to love in truth and to be truthful in love. We pray in Jesus' name. Amen.

The Questions

- When we find a fine-sounding argument we consider suspect or specious, how do we avoid leveling a personal attack against the teacher?
- Have you ever been deceived by a fine-sounding argument that seemed true at the time but later proved suspect? How did you handle that?
- Have you come to grips with your susceptibility to be deceived? If not, do you recognize this in itself makes you highly susceptible to be deceived?

13 How the Way Is Made by Walking (on Water)

COLOSSIANS 2:6–7 NRSV | As you therefore have received Christ Jesus the Lord, continue to live your lives in him, rooted and built up in him and established in the faith, just as you were taught, abounding in thanksgiving.

Consider This

For the longest time I interpreted this text to mean something like, "Go to the gym." It is hard to overestimate the depth of our formation (particularly as twenty-first-century

Americans) in self-help thinking. Our inner mantra, whether we are conscious of it or not, is, "I think I can." Love them or hate them, we tend to live by those ten most powerful two-letter words, "If it is to be, it is up to me." And to be sure, in most of life the mantra holds true.

If I want to get in physical shape, it is up to me to stop eating Swiss cake rolls for breakfast and go to the gym instead. It stands to reason, does it not, that if I want to get in spiritual shape, I must wake up earlier, read more Scripture, pray longer, and fast more regularly?

No.

"As you therefore have received Christ Jesus the Lord . . ." (v. 6a). So, how did we receive Christ Jesus as Lord? Was that by our effort and strength and willpower? No, it was by grace through faith. Yes, it was a decisive turning of our hearts, minds, strength, and wills to Jesus, but we didn't bring anything to the table in any sort of quid pro quo arrangement. We freely received. So now what?

. . . continue to live your lives in him . . . (v. 6b)

The Greek word there is *peripateo* (per-ee-pat-eh-o). It is an ordinary, everyday kind of word that means "to walk around." In researching this my attention was strangely drawn to Matthew 14:29, which says: "'Come,' he said. Then Peter got down out of the boat, walked on the water and came toward Jesus."

How perfect is this? Peter could try walking on water for a thousand years. He could practice it, perfect his technique, and fail a thousand out of a thousand tries. And then Jesus says something like, "Come on!" and Peter steps out of the boat and it happens.

This way is made by walking, though it is a different kind of walking altogether. This way Jesus calls us to walk is not about our effort, technique, or spiritual work ethic. So often, in doing these things we unknowingly put our faith in these things. This walk is by grace through faith. It doesn't begin with our activity but our receptivity.

What if we thought of our spiritual practice not as walking around a track but as walking on water? What if each morning we saw ourselves not as settling into our favorite chair to read the Bible but as standing up in the boat and preparing to walk over the edge, onto the water? (Honestly, that's what it feels like to write the Daily Text. You can blame the misses on me, but every one that hits can be credited to Jesus.)

I think this is what it looks like for us to be "rooted and built up in him and established in the faith, just as you were taught, abounding in thanksgiving" (v. 7 NRSV).

We aren't building ourselves up through our activity. We are being built up in the gift of receptivity, which always begins with the giver. I have waded around in the shallow end of my own activity enough to now know the difference. This is what grace through faith looks like.

The Prayer

Abba Father, we thank you for your Son, Jesus, who ever stands on the water and beckons us to "Come on!" Remind me that all of my activity while still in the boat is still just my activity. Come, Holy Spirit, and awaken faith in me to walk out onto the water. I can't muster this up. I must receive it. I am ready. We pray in Jesus' name. Amen.

The Questions

- How do you relate to this notion of walking on water as the everyday practice and experience of our faith versus sitting back in the boat, busy with activity but still in the boat?
- How deep does the self-help mentality go in you? Or, I should say, how deep is your awareness of this mentality in you?
- Do you ever feel as if you must build yourself up with your spiritual activity in order for God to be with you?

When Philosophy Hates Wisdom

14

COLOSSIANS 2:8 NRSV | See to it that no one takes you captive through philosophy and empty deceit, according to human tradition, according to the elemental spirits of the universe, and not according to Christ.

Consider This

There's a real irony when philosophy hates wisdom. After all, you know what the word means. *Philo* means love, and *sophy* means wisdom.

I have spent about half of my life inside the cavernous confines of academia. I do not eschew scholarship but highly value it; however, I find much that poses as scholarship to be an endless exercise in the deceptive vanity of competitive speculation. Most of our universities have long since abandoned the quest for godly wisdom, as have, sadly, so many of our seminaries. Twenty-five years ago, I found one of the good ones and never left it.

All this to say, I think I get what Paul is getting at here.

> See to it that no one takes you captive through philosophy and empty deceit, according to human tradition, according to the elemental spirits of the universe, and not according to Christ. (v. 8 NRSV)

Paul has already appealed to the word "wisdom" three times and will do so once more before the letter is signed (1:9; 1:28; 2:3; 3:16). The wisdom of the world can be very seductive, inviting the mind on a noble quest that turns out to be a hall of mirrors. I have witnessed too many people get caught up in it, turn away from God, shipwreck their faith, and in its place develop an impenetrable cynicism of resistance. It parades itself in age-old mantras like, "Philosophy is questions that may never be answered. Religion is answers that may never be questioned."

I remember as a young university student being baited toward the alluring abyss of atheism. I providentially came across Francis Bacon's piercing quote in his essay "Of Atheists": "It is true, that a little philosophy inclineth man's mind to atheism; but depth in philosophy bringeth men's minds about to religion."

Jesus Christ is the wisdom of God. I love how Paul put it to the Corinthians:

> Where is the one who is wise? Where is the scribe? Where is the debater of this age? Has not God made foolish the wisdom of the world? For since, in the wisdom of God, the world did not know God through wisdom, God decided, through the foolishness of our proclamation, to save those who believe. (1 Cor. 1:20–21 NRSV)

We need not become anti-academic, and we certainly need not despise learning and the quest for knowledge. So often Christians can be bullied with the attack of being narrow-minded as though open-mindedness were somehow a more virtuous option. What we must have is sound-mindedness. This way is found in Jesus, who is our wisdom and who would lead us into a wisdom worthy of our highest love and most noble aspirations—indeed, the very mind of Christ, the living way of the holy cross.

Giving Paul the last word:

For the message about the cross is foolishness to those who are perishing, but to us who are being saved it is the power of God. For it is written,

"I will destroy the wisdom of the wise,
and the discernment of the discerning I will thwart." . . .

For God's foolishness is wiser than human wisdom, and God's weakness is stronger than human strength. (1 Cor. 1:18–19, 25 NRSV)

Domino #2|8 tends to show up in that freshman philosophy class, which unfortunately poses as continuing education all along the way. Watch out for it. It can be another reverse tipper.

The Prayer

Abba Father, we thank you for your Son, Jesus, who is our wisdom. Grant me the gift of the mind of Christ that I might be able to discern wisdom and to know what is true and best in all situations. Lead me in the way not of higher learning but of the highest learning. We pray in Jesus' name. Amen.

The Questions

- Have you ever been caught up in or taken captive by hollow and deceptive philosophy?
- What does it mean to you that Jesus is your wisdom?

- How do you understand the difference between narrow-mindedness, open-mindedness, and sound-mindedness?

The Change That Could Change Everything for Us

15

COLOSSIANS 2:9–10 | For in Christ all the fullness of the Deity lives in bodily form, and in Christ you have been brought to fullness. He is the head over every power and authority.

Consider This

For me, these are among the most extraordinary and powerful words in all of the Bible:

> For in Christ all the fullness of the Deity lives in bodily form, and in Christ you have been brought to fullness. (vv. 9–10a)

Notice the verb tense. All the fullness of God lives in bodily form in Christ. God now lives completely and totally yet not exclusively (because there's also the Father and the Spirit, in whom also the fullness of God lives completely and totally). This has been happening in the past and is now happening in the present. Now note the past tense in verse 10: "in Christ you have been brought to fullness." It is done, an accomplished reality.

The big question for us Christians is: Are we living in this reality, or are we still waiting on something else to happen? If we are not living in this reality, it stands to reason we are not real Christians. I know that sounds harsh, but sometimes we need to be confronted with the plain truth of Scripture. So how about it? Are you living in the reality of the fullness of God in your life, or are you still waiting on something else to happen?

What if I told you I put $100,000 in a special account at your bank last night, and what if I told you it wouldn't show up on your online banking app or on your bank statement? The only way you could access the money would be to spend it by writing a check or by using your debit card. What would you do?

Today's text is effectively telling us that we have all the fullness of God in our spiritual bank accounts in our physical bodies. God is not waiting on us to do something. He's waiting on us to write the check, to spend the funds, to move in faith on the fact of his fullness being present right now.

The fundamental shift so desperately needed in our discipleship today is the movement from what we need God to do for us to moving out in faith on what God has already done.

> . . . and in Christ you have been brought to fullness.
> (v. 10a)

We must make a bold shift in our faith from, "Fill me with the fullness of God," to "I am filled with the fullness of God."

Domino #2|10, The Fullness of God, cries out in every age to be tipped over. It is a mountain mover.

On your mark. Get set. Go!

The Prayer

Abba Father, we thank you for your Son, Jesus, in whom dwells all the fullness of God in bodily form. Thank you for making us alive in him and pouring out his fullness into our lives. I confess I struggle with this. I believe it, yet I do not act on it. I keep asking, and yet I hear you saying, "It's already done. Now move out on it." I will. We pray in Jesus' name. Amen.

The Questions

- How about you? Are you living in the reality of the fullness of God, or still asking God to do it?
- What do you think it will mean for you to make this shift from "Fill me with your fullness," to "I am filled with your fullness"?
- Could part of the problem be that you are trying to go it alone, that you aren't closely enough related to other believers going on this journey?

16 On the Difference between Difficult and Impossible

COLOSSIANS 2:11–12 | In him you were also circumcised with a circumcision not performed by human hands. Your whole self ruled by the flesh was put off when you were circumcised by Christ, having been buried with him in baptism, in which you were also raised with him through your faith in the working of God, who raised him from the dead.

Consider This

The Christian life, or as Paul will describe it to the Colossians, the life "hidden with Christ in God" (Col. 3:3), is not difficult. It is impossible. Maybe this is our biggest problem. We think it is difficult, and because of this, we resolve ourselves to try harder. When we come up short again and again, we consider it too difficult and settle back in to a life of easy believism, cheap grace, and self-satisfied, mediocre, compromised existence.

The Christian life is not difficult. This would be to evaluate it on our terms. The Christian life is impossible. It does not require more effort on a human level. It requires the movement to an eternal level of living. Jesus' invitation to us is not meant to elicit more resolve but deeper surrender. It's why he said things like, "Come to me, all you who are weary and burdened, and I will give you rest. Take my yoke upon you and learn from me, for I am gentle and humble in heart, and you will find rest for your souls. For my yoke is easy and my burden is light" (Matt. 11:28–30).

Paul wants to awaken us not to the possibility of redemption but to the fact of it: "Your whole self ruled by the flesh was put off when you were circumcised by Christ" (v. 2:11b).

Circumcision was the mark of the old covenant. Baptism is the mark of the new covenant. While baptism is an outward sign, it signifies something decisively done by the very hand of God—the circumcision of the heart.

> Your whole self ruled by the flesh was put off when you were circumcised by Christ, having been buried with him in baptism, in which you were also raised with him through your faith in the working of God, who raised him from the dead. (vv. 11b–12)

My faith in the working of God, who raised Jesus from the dead, must translate into my faith in the working of God, who raised me from the dead, and all the incredible implications of such a resurrection. This is the plane of eternal life. This is the substance of real Christianity.

We happen to be living in an era of human history and even church history where real Christianity has been traded in for a cheap substitute, an easy counterfeit. It should be no surprise that this coincides with the rise of a generation who characterizes their religious affiliation with the word *none*. They are the "nones." What this means is they will have none of the brand of faith we are offering. Can we blame them? They want something authentic. Though they don't know it, what they want is real Christianity.

Who will show it to them? Whoever will awaken to the fact of an already accomplished redemption and the necessity of a few other people to help them receive this death-and-resurrection-real-Christian-reality fully into their lives.

The Prayer

Abba Father, we thank you for your Son, Jesus, who not only has done it, but who *is* it. He is our redemption. He is our death and our resurrection. Awaken me to my life hidden with Christ in God and your readiness to reveal it to others through me. We pray in Jesus' name. Amen.

The Questions

- Could our struggle to live the Christian life be connected to the lack of a deep reality of Christ in us?
- Could the shallowness of "Christ in me" be connected to a lack of deep faith-formational relationships with others?
- What does it mean to you to awaken, not to the possibility of redemption, but to the fact of it, and to move from endless struggle with sin to victory over sin?

On the Difference between Sin, Sins, and Credit Card Debt

17

COLOSSIANS 2:13–15 NRSV | And when you were dead in trespasses and the uncircumcision of your flesh, God made you alive together with him, when he forgave us all our trespasses, erasing the record that stood against us with its legal demands. He set this aside, nailing it to the cross. He disarmed the rulers and authorities and made a public example of them, triumphing over them in it.

Consider This

In law school I learned two rival conceptions of reality that I have forever mixed up until now. The terms are *de jure* and *de facto*. *De jure* means "of law." *De facto* means "of fact." Something can be true of law, yet not be true of fact.

A couple can be married de facto and not be married de jure, though it is unfortunately more often the opposite. Consider the difference between de facto sovereignty and de jure sovereignty. Though Jesus is the true, or de jure Sovereign over our lives, sin manages to hold on to rogue, or de facto, sovereignty in our experience. Why is this?

How could this be, given this word from today's text?

And when you were dead in trespasses and the uncircumcision of your flesh, God made you alive together

with him, when he forgave us all our trespasses, erasing
the record that stood against us with its legal demands.
He set this aside, nailing it to the cross. (vv. 13–14 NRSV)

I think it is because we don't understand the difference
between sins and sin. Do you see the distinction in the
text? There are "our trespasses," and there is our legal
indebtedness. We are not in debt because of our sins. We
are in debt because of sin. To be sure, our sins have added
to our debt, as the interest on a debt adds to the debt, but
our legal indebtedness is sin itself. It has stood against us
from Eden and condemned us from the moment we were
born. If I've said it once on the Daily Text, I've said it a
hundred times: we aren't sinners because we sin. We sin
because we are sinners.

As I write, I have a credit card debt that I can't pay back
at the moment. Every month the bill comes back around,
and I have a choice. I can pay any amount I want, from the
minimum to the whole thing. Know what happens? Because
I can't pay it off, I usually pay some approximation of the
minimum (which may cover some portion of the interest),
because there are other bills that don't permit such a slavish
privilege. You too? Now, regardless of my payment, the debt
keeps going up, and with that the payment.

Are you seeing the analogy to sin and sins? I get that Jesus
has paid my legal indebtedness. I am de jure out of debt. So
why do I keep making the de facto payment? When we keep
on sinning, we effectively pay the interest on a debt that no

longer exists. This is why Jesus probably spends a lot of time scratching his head!

Have you ever been to a note- or mortgage-burning ceremony? It's a beautiful thing to see the record of legal indebtedness go up in smoke before our very eyes. Well, this is exactly what the cross was and is and forevermore shall be.

> He disarmed the rulers and authorities and made a public example of them, triumphing over them in it.
> (v. 15 NRSV)

The note on our sin, the record of our legal indebtedness, has been canceled—nailed to the cross, no less. Reminds me of the third stanza of the classic hymn "It Is Well with My Soul" by Horatio G. Spafford:

> My sin—oh, the bliss of this glorious thought!—
> My sin, not in part but the whole,
> Is nailed to the cross, and I bear it no more,
> Praise the Lord, praise the Lord, O my soul!

Domino #2|14, let's call it The Mortgage Burner.

The Prayer

Abba Father, we thank you for your Son, Jesus, the Lamb of God, who takes away the sin of the world. Awaken me to my sin, and help me understand the difference between my sin and my sins. Come, Holy Spirit, and witness to this gospel to my own soul. We pray in Jesus' name. Amen.

The Questions

- Have you looked upon the cross and seen, not just your sins, but your sin? See the difference?
- Have you ever preached this gospel of Colossians 2:13–15 to yourself or to those brothers or sisters with whom you are banded together?
- Are you still paying interest on a debt that no longer in law exists? Why?

18 | Why We Trade in the Movement for the Motions

COLOSSIANS 2:16–17 ESV | Therefore let no one pass judgment on you in questions of food and drink, or with regard to a festival or a new moon or a Sabbath. These are a shadow of the things to come, but the substance belongs to Christ.

Consider This

Near the end of his life, John Wesley once famously said of the movement he helped to found:

I am not afraid that the people called Methodists should ever cease to exist either in Europe or America. But I am afraid lest they should only exist as a dead sect, having the form of religion without the power.

> And this undoubtedly will be the case unless they hold
> fast both the doctrine, spirit, and discipline with which
> they first set out.[1]

Form without power . . . ritual without reality . . . motions
without movement . . . these signify the kiss of death for the
work of God in a community of people. Forms and rituals
and motions can be good things until they become the main
things, denying the dynamics they were created to cultivate.

> Therefore let no one pass judgment on you in ques-
> tions of food and drink, or with regard to a festival or
> a new moon or a Sabbath. These are a shadow of the
> things to come, but the substance belongs to Christ.
> (Col. 2:16–17 ESV)

It seems as though some people from First Methodist on
Main Street visited the Colossians Community Church across
town and told them they weren't doing it right. They must
have been mortified at the absence of a bulletin announcing
the "New Moon celebration" and upcoming Sabbath
non-activities.

Paul will not have it. He knows the difference between the
Tradition and the traditions and how well-meaning people
will sometimes unwittingly and other times knowingly trade
in the former for the latter. Hear him clearly when he says,
"but the substance belongs to Christ."

---

1   John Wesley, "Thoughts upon Methodism," reprinted in *One Methodist* 2, no. 2
(September 1999), http://www.imarc.cc/one_meth/vol-02-no-02.html.

You know the difference. Tradition is the living faith of the dead. Traditionalism is the dead faith of the living. How does this happen? It all begins with this great mystery of our faith, "Christ has died. Christ is risen. Christ will come again." The reality is found in Christ, and Christ must be found in us.

The mystery gets translated into a message that begets messengers. Movement is born. A way of working with the mystery emerges in the form of shared movements (e.g., the Lord's Supper, etc.). These movements help us remember together and, done well, they lead us to experience the great mystery together. Over time, however, the movements that helped us move with the Movement slowly become the motions. Before long, entire communities and even denominations become focused on the motions. Somewhere along the way, the motions get passed on without their meanings, and they get disconnected from the movement, at which point we find ourselves simply "going through the motions." We find ourselves with a form of religion without the power, rituals without the reality, and motions without the movement.

In response, some leaders will advocate throwing out the motions. It's another post, but often leaders will reach for e-motions instead (which are not bad but can unwittingly counterfeit the reality we seek). I think the best leaders work to reconnect the motions to the movement again, which must begin with the core mystery—Christ in us.

There are many pitfalls on the path to real Christianity. We must develop a dogged determination to settle for nothing less.

Domino #2|16 posts another warning for us to beware of motions that aren't connected to movement.

The Prayer

Abba Father, we thank you for your Son, Jesus, who is both the form and the power, in whose death and resurrection are both the ritual and the reality, and in whose body are both the mystery and the movement. I want the reality, Lord. Lead me into the reality. I must have the reality. We pray in Jesus' name. Amen.

The Questions

- How do you relate to this notion of form without power, ritual without reality, and motion without movement?
- How do people become so loyal to the motions at the cost of the movement and the loss of the mystery? Has this ever happened to you?
- Have you come to a dogged determination to live in "the reality" at whatever cost and come what may? May be time to look up Jeremiah 29:13 again.

19 Beware of Super-Spiritual People and Communities

COLOSSIANS 2:18–19 | Do not let anyone who delights in false humility and the worship of angels disqualify you. Such a person also goes into great detail about what they have seen; they are puffed up with idle notions by their unspiritual mind. They have lost connection with the head, from whom the whole body, supported and held together by its ligaments and sinews, grows as God causes it to grow.

Consider This

A wise professor of theology once remarked to me to beware of people who profess special revelation from God. He said the more "spiritual" things get, the more dangerous and even demonic they become. Today's text reminds me of that conversation so many years ago.

One of the challenges these early churches dealt with was the heresy of Gnosticism. Gnostics claimed they had received special revelation from God. This knowledge set them apart from ordinary Christians and became a source of power and elitism for them. Such persons also go into great detail about what they have seen; they are puffed up with idle notions by their unspiritual minds. The irony is how these people, whom Paul calls "unspiritual," become known as ultra-spiritual people.

The mark of a spiritual person, in the tradition of Jesus, is not some kind of super-spirituality but the holiness of his or her humanity. Jesus did not become a human being so that we could become something other than or more than human beings. He became a human being so that we could embody the holiness of humanity.

Paul warns the Colossians and he warns us today to be wary of super-spiritual people and super-spiritual communities. These people and groups tend to define themselves not by the revelation of the gospel common to us all, but by extra revelations and special teaching. You have to go there and to them to get it. Only certain teachers and leaders are anointed to share it. And because it often gets framed in orthodox biblical categories and the language of supernatural dimensions, it can be so alluring and seem so right.

Paul said one of the hallmarks of such persons and communities is false humility. People who "delight in false humility" do so by putting themselves on a higher plane than others. They claim to be humbled to receive such revelation, which ironically serves as a veil to mask their pride in being so chosen.

The hallmark of real Christianity is not elevation but descent. It is not revealed through people who venture higher up, aspiring for more spiritual experiences, but those who journey downward, ever increasing their experience of loving and serving others.

> They have lost connection with the head, from whom
> the whole body, supported and held together by its liga-
> ments and sinews, grows as God causes it to grow. (v. 19)

What we need is Jesus, our Head, and we can only be connected to him through his body, the church. God is growing the church. God is not searching for super-spiritual people to grow the church, but for ordinary saints.

That's Domino #2|18; another warning sign: beware of the super-spiritual. They tip all right, just not in the right direction.

The Prayer

Abba Father, we thank you for your Son, Jesus, in whose image we are made and on whom we fix our gaze, for it is only in beholding him that we can become like him. I renounce my own quest for super-spiritual status. I want to be a holy human being, one in whom you are pleased to dwell and through whom you delight in revealing yourself. We pray in Jesus' name. Amen.

The Questions

- Have you ever been around people (and/or communi-ties) who set themselves apart by their own experiences of God, humbly claiming a kind of super-spiritual status? Were you drawn to follow and become like them?

- What do you make of this notion that the more "spiritual" something or someone is, the more dangerous he or she (or it) becomes?
- What do you observe about the ways Jesus teaches and demonstrates what it means to be spiritual?

Are You a Rule Follower or a Rule Breaker?

20

COLOSSIANS 2:20–23 NRSV | If with Christ you died to the elemental spirits of the universe, why do you live as if you still belonged to the world? Why do you submit to regulations, "Do not handle, Do not taste, Do not touch"? All these regulations refer to things that perish with use; they are simply human commands and teachings. These have indeed an appearance of wisdom in promoting self-imposed piety, humility, and severe treatment of the body, but they are of no value in checking self-indulgence.

Consider This

Rules don't work. Of course, they are necessary and they have value, but if they are all we have, we don't have much. Rules can protect us from ourselves and each other. They can create some semblance of external order, but they do not change people. Rules can govern human behavior, but they have no power to order the affairs of our minds and hearts.

People often identify themselves as being either rule followers or rule breakers, and both with equal degrees of pride. We do not need rules. What we need is a Ruler. The lordship of Jesus Christ has nothing to do with following the rules and everything to do with following the Ruler.

This way of following the Ruler is the way of the cross—the path of death and resurrection. Note how today's text begins, "If with Christ you died . . ." (v. 20a NRSV). To die with Christ means we have renounced self-rule and surrendered ourselves to the person of Jesus. FULL STOP.

Most self-avowed Christians have never done this. They have, instead, adopted a form of Christian faith without the power. Consider how we talk about becoming a Christian. We speak of one accepting Christ, as though we were accepting a software agreement online. Where is this in the Bible? It is minimalism.

If one was a rule keeper before he accepted Christ, then he becomes a legalistic Christian. If one was a rule breaker before, then she becomes a licentious Christian. Neither has changed. No, they have merely baptized their way of life in Jesus' name. There is no orientation to the Ruler, only to the rules.

Paul is dealing with a community of people who want to be real Christians but who are getting caught in all the predictable traps. These traps are as operative now as they were then. There are the philosophers and their fine-sounding arguments; the super-spiritualists and their special revelations; the rule followers and the rule breakers; the conservatives and the liberals.

Paul knows we are dealing with something far deeper than human behavior. He knows the rules hold no power against self-indulgence and the seductive wiles of our appetites. He knows only the presence of the Ruler himself in the depths of our innermost selves can transform the human mind and heart. He knows death and resurrection is the only way.

Domino #2|20 moves us from the rules to the Ruler, preparing the way for mountain-moving movement.

The Prayer

Abba Father, we thank you for your Son, Jesus, who leads us in the way of death that we might find truth of resurrection and live from the depths of the very life of God in our deepest selves. I cannot find this way apart from you. Please take me by the hand and lead me in this way, every day of my life. We pray in Jesus' name. Amen.

The Questions

- So how about it . . . are you a rule follower or a rule breaker? What do you learn about yourself from that? Ever notice how rule breakers and rule followers each think they are superior to the other? Why is that?
- What do you make of this difference between death-and-resurrection Christians and those who merely baptize their old way of life in Jesus' name?

- Have you renounced self-rule and surrendered your life to the person of Jesus Christ? Is it time to get back in touch with that surrender?

21 How to Move from Morning Devotions to Movemental Devotions

COLOSSIANS 3:1–2 | Since, then, you have been raised with Christ, set your hearts on things above, where Christ is, seated at the right hand of God. Set your minds on things above, not on earthly things.

Consider This

Can we grapple a bit together today? I want us to honestly ask ourselves and one another how we do this?

> [S]et your hearts on things above, where Christ is, seated at the right hand of God. Set your minds on things above, not on earthly things. (vv. 1b–2)

Is reading a couple of devotional entries a day supposed to do this for us? Is this a matter of thinking about Jesus for a few minutes every morning? If I'm honest, and I look at my own life, that's what it comes down to. Sure, I think about Jesus throughout the day. I pray without ceasing sometimes, but Colossians 3:1–2 seems to be asking for something a bit more comprehensive and engaging.

I have written before about the Christian life being much more about receptivity than activity, and I stand by that. The life hid with Christ in God is not about amping up our activity but deepening our receptivity. So, what does receptivity look like? It surely must mean more than a few minutes of reading spiritual things and thinking about Jesus. Receptivity looks like this:

> Since, then, you have been raised with Christ, set your hearts on things above, where Christ is, seated at the right hand of God. Set your minds on things above, not on earthly things. (Col. 3:1–2)

I think athletes get this more than the average person does. Athletes have a pregame routine they stick to with religious fervor. It is completely embodied with physical, mental, spiritual, and social elements. Watch a professional golfer in his pre-shot ritual. Observe the consistency of a field-goal kicker on the football field before the kick. Note the idiosyncratic and even superstitious gestures of a baseball pitcher before every single pitch. The best athletes are distinguished by their ability to wed a type of meditative, futuristic visualization with a preprogrammed form of muscle memory to reach extraordinary levels of performance and achievement.

There's a word that captures this kind of focus: *devotion*. I think the insight my grappling is leading me to is the following: we have traded devotion for devotions. I'm afraid we've gotten a lot better at delighting ourselves with restful morning devotions than we are at the movemental discipline of rigorous devotion.

Maybe it's time we took a break from our morning devotions and came up with something more like a pregame warm-up, or a pre-day ritual. Maybe we are doing the right kinds of motions, but we need to reconnect them to the movement again. It's about resetting our hearts and minds. What if we thought of our day as the game and our schedule as the field of faith? What would it mean to peer through the lens of our calendar at the ascended Lord Jesus Christ?

When the Holy Spirit calls you to "set your hearts on things above, where Christ is, seated at the right hand of God," and to "set your minds on things above, not on earthly things," he's not asking if you did morning devotions. No, he's calling us to another plane of devotion.

That's Domino #3|1, Focus.

The Prayer

Abba Father, we thank you for your Son, Jesus, in whose life we see pure devotion. Come, Holy Spirit, and awaken me to the thinness of my devotions, and awaken me to fix my gaze on the Devoted One, that I may learn to become like him. We pray in Jesus' name. Amen.

The Questions

- How about it? Are your devotions leading to devotion, or are they just more devotions?

- What's your pregame/pre-day warm-up look like?
- How does this call to set your mind and heart on things above challenge you today? How will you respond? What experiment in devotion will you try today?

How You Can Go to Your Own Funeral

22

COLOSSIANS 3:3–4 | For you died, and your life is now hidden with Christ in God. When Christ, who is your life, appears, then you also will appear with him in glory.

Consider This

The one thing we will never be able to do is attend our own funerals. We will be there, all right. It's just that we won't *be there* be there. It's why we should spend a lot more time eulogizing the living, but I digress.

That's what is so revolutionary about today's text. Paul tells us we must host our own funerals, behold ourselves being laid in the ground and buried, and then keep coming back to the cemetery and visiting the tombstone in order to remind ourselves.

> For you died, and your life is now hidden with Christ in God. (v. 3)

Here's a life application point for you. Get yourself a dry-erase marker and write Colossians 3:3 on your bathroom mirror:

> For you died, and your life is now hidden with Christ in God. (Col. 3:3)

If ever there were a verse that needed to jump off the page and into our days, this is it. As I pointed out the decade-long focus our team had with Colossians 2:2 a week or so back (remember the 2|2 Domino?), I am only today discovering the serendipity of 3|3. Now that's a domino effect!

Because he knows the secret to life is to die before you die, Paul wants us to attend our own funerals. There is a technical term for this phenomenon: baptism.

Paul summarized it brilliantly in his letter to the Romans:

> Or don't you know that all of us who were baptized into Christ Jesus were baptized into his death? We were therefore buried with him through baptism into death in order that, just as Christ was raised from the dead through the glory of the Father, we too may live a new life. (Rom. 6:3–4)

There are many metaphors and meanings for Christian baptism, but for my money, there is increasingly only one: death and resurrection. Talk about reconnecting the motions to the movement—we must begin here!

I get and support baptizing babies, but only if the rite of confirmation could involve a casket—which is probably why

I haven't been asked to pastor a local church. I also support services of baptismal remembrance, but only if they involve holding one's breath while under water. What we need are not more baptismal rituals and remembrances for the spiritually dead. What we need are more tombstones for the living. And here's the epitaph: "For you died, and your life is now hidden with Christ in God" (Col. 3:3).

Let's call Domino #3|3: The Funeral.

The Prayer

Abba Father, we thank you for your Son, Jesus, who precedes us in the only death worth dying and in the only life worth living. Teach me the secret of dying before I die, that I might truly live while I am alive. And we thank you that because of Jesus, we can die before we die such that we will not die when we die but be alive forevermore. We pray in Jesus' name. Amen.

The Questions

- Have you been to your own funeral yet? Why not?
- What do you remember about your own baptism? It didn't have to be a grand experience at the time. It can actually be retrofitted with its real meaning. What might that look like?
- Have you written Colossians 3:3 on your bathroom mirror in dry-erase ink yet? What are you waiting for?

23 The Difference between a Death Sentence and the Death Penalty

COLOSSIANS 3:5–6 | Put to death, therefore, whatever belongs to your earthly nature: sexual immorality, impurity, lust, evil desires and greed, which is idolatry. Because of these, the wrath of God is coming.

Consider This

Whether you are a supporter of the death penalty or not, I need you to think through the metaphor for purposes of today's Daily Text.

There's the death sentence and then there's the actual death penalty. Once a person is given the death penalty, he is exiled to death row, where he waits to be taken to the execution chamber, at which point he is actually put to death. People can wait on death row for years, exhausting a long appeals process and such, before they are actually put to death.

It's an apt metaphor, for isn't this exactly the way we deal with sin in our lives? Because Jesus has died to sin once and for all, sin is now on death row. It has no power other than the rogue power we grant it in our own lives.

In death penalty parlance, the distance between death row and the death chamber is called the last mile. And though it is undoubtedly much shorter than an actual mile, it must feel like the most difficult mile of them all.

It has me thinking today about what it would mean to visit death row in my own soul and walk past the prisoners. What sins are locked up there, awaiting execution? I think I know, but have I identified and named them? That's what Paul is doing in today's text:

> Put to death, therefore, whatever belongs to your earthly nature: sexual immorality, impurity, lust, evil desires and greed, which is idolatry. (v. 5)

What would it mean to walk that last mile, escorting my sins to the death chamber? How many times have you walked your sins to the death chamber only to walk them back to the cell again?

Part of the problem is the way we are conditioned to think about the death penalty. We tend to think in terms of something quick and relatively painless, like a lethal injection. When Paul speaks of "putting to death," he's thinking of the cross. We must crucify our sins, which can be a slow, arduous, and agonizing death.

I think the main reason we fail to put our sins to death is we try to walk that last mile alone. Condemned, canceled sin can be so wily and deceptive, and it can keep us shrouded in so much shame that we can't bear even the thought of opening up about it to someone else. That is what a band is for—not to put you down but to lift you up; not to shame you but to honor you in the struggle.

There's that fantastic scene near the end of *The Return of the King*, the last epic of the *Lord of the Rings* trilogy. Samwise and Frodo had come to proverbial last mile. Frodo had carried the horrifically deceptive ring of power all this way and was finally collapsing in failure on the brink of victory. The immortal words of Samwise Gamgee to Frodo Baggins capture what it so often takes to get us through the last mile from death row to the death chamber, "Then let us be rid of it, once and for all! Come on, Mr. Frodo. I can't carry it for you, but I can carry you!"

Domino #3|5 shall be called Death Chamber.

The Prayer

Abba Father, we thank you for your Son, Jesus, who not only carried our sin to the cross, but who carries us. Awaken me to the deception in my soul about my own sins. Thank you for exiling my sins to death row. Now come, Holy Spirit, and help me finally put them to death, one by one. And raise up a band around me to help. We pray in Jesus' name. Amen.

The Questions

- How do you relate to this metaphor of the last mile between death row and the death chamber?
- Can you name the inmates (sin) on death row in your innermost self? Are you tired of visiting them? Are you ready to be done with them once and for all?

- Would you be willing to share these struggles with your band in confidence? Would you be willing to pray about starting or joining a band? You will be in good company with many who are already on the path.

Why Anger Management Will Never Get It Done

COLOSSIANS 3:7–8 | You used to walk in these ways, in the life you once lived. But now you must also rid yourselves of all such things as these: anger, rage, malice, slander, and filthy language from your lips.

Consider This

"You used to walk in these ways, in the life you once lived. . . ."

Paul had never been to Colossae. He didn't actually know these Colossians, but he knew Jesus. And he knew that when Jesus enters a person's life, everything changes.

We all have a "life [we] once lived." We all "used to walk in these ways." It's good, from time to time, to take stock of the change in our lives. What are the ways you used to walk in the "life you once lived"? How would you describe the ways you walk in today?

OK, I'll go first. I used to be a really angry person. You would have never known it because I spent a lot of energy keeping it at bay. Only the people closest to me would have had a sense of my anger. And the crazy thing about anger is you aren't really angry about what you are angry about. You know what I'm talking about?

Anger is a normal human emotion—until it takes root in your inmost self. Then it becomes like malignant cancer. Anger unbridled becomes rage. Anger imprisoned within becomes depression. It can be really complex, but the primary source of anger is pain. You don't get rid of anger by trying to not be angry. You have to deal with your pain. Anger is pain's wounded ambassador.

What does it look like to rid ourselves of our particular sin propensities? My journey toward ridding myself of anger was long and complex, but I think there may be a general pattern and progression that can be helpful for other issues.

First, and for the longest time, I was unaware of my anger issues. Somewhere along the way, by the grace of God (and a little help from my friends—also the grace of God), I became *self-aware*. Then, because I began to understand how my anger was hurting others, I started to *care*. I realized how powerless I was against this volcanic force within me. As noted, trying harder to not be angry did not work. It made me angrier. At that point I began to pull out my *hair* (not literally) and *swear* (see also "filthy language" from the list above). Are you feeling my rhyme scheme yet?

Throughout this process I was meeting regularly with a few trusted friends who were listening and praying with me. I sought the help of a counselor, who helped me identify and delve into the deeper sources of my pain, which led me into a process of forgiveness. Further, this led me to work with a pastor friend of mine who led me through a process of deliverance *prayer*. (Catch that rhyme?)

All of this brings me to the final rhyme in the scheme of this journey of riddance—*share*. God shared his nature with me, which is love. From beginning to end it was the love of God that delivered me from anger, and when anger is touched by love, it becomes love. Anger management, like any other form of sin management, will never get it done.

So, there you have it—the life I once lived—from unaware to self-aware to beginning to care to pulling out my hair to the temptation to swear to healing prayer to God's decision to share. We want it to be so much simpler and quicker, and sometimes it is. The cross always has a will of its own, and it is always for God's glory and our good.

Do I ever get angry anymore? Of course. Like everyone else, I have anger. Anger just doesn't have me anymore.

Riddance. It's a good name for Domino #3|8.

The Prayer

Abba Father, we thank you for your Son, Jesus, who not only shows us the way of the cross but who walks every step of the way with us. Open my eyes to the sin I am unaware of, and lead me on the grace-filled journey of riddance, for your glory and my good. We pray in Jesus' name. Amen.

The Questions

- How about you? Can you articulate the life you once lived and the ways particular sins defined your walk?
- How did the process of riddance go for you? How do you relate to the pattern I outlined?
- Is there a sin pattern or even a besetting sin you would like to move into a full-fledged riddance process? What is holding you back?

25 Breaking Free from the Slavery of Your Old Self

COLOSSIANS 3:9–10 NRSV | Do not lie to one another, seeing that you have stripped off the old self with its practices and have clothed yourselves with the new self, which is being renewed in knowledge according to the image of its creator.

My Medatative discoveries are renewals in knowledge through the devine - God.

Consider This

Have you realized there are at least two versions of you? Today's text references these two versions as the "old self" and the "new self." Another way of stating it would be the false self and the true self. The false self is the image of ourselves that we manage to cobble together over time to generate a sense of identity and self-worth (or not). The new, or true, self is the image of God alive or waiting to be awakened in our inmost being.

Real Christianity is the journey from the old or false self to the new or true self. Until we embark on this journey, we are destined to live a lie. Isn't this what the text is saying?

> Do not lie to one another, seeing that you have stripped off the old self with its practices and have clothed yourselves with the new self, which is being renewed in knowledge according to the image of its creator. (vv. 9–10 NRSV)

Unfortunately, so many people live so much of their lives unaware of these things. Lying to one another does not mean telling untruths to each other; rather, it means projecting an image of yourself to other people that simply is not true. Most people do not intend to do this. They can't help it. One's outward image is a direct projection of his or her inward sense of identity and when this identity is built on things that are not true (i.e., anything other than the image of God), that individual's outward image lies about who he or she most deeply is.

We have all known people whose outward physical appearance is a marvel to behold. So often, people who focus great energy on their outward appearance believe their value as a person is directly related to their appearance. As a result, some of the most physically attractive people in the world are the most deeply insecure about their appearance. Worse, they often believe they are unattractive. The internal lies drive them to, in effect, create an external image they can't even believe themselves. Similarly, many financially wealthy people live from the lie of scarcity at the core of their sense of self. No matter how much they accumulate, it will never be enough.

The old or false self creates the conditions known as slavery. We become ensnared by the lies we believe about ourselves, and those lies enslave us to practices whereby we try to convince ourselves and others that the direct opposite is true of us. In other words, the reason we spend so much of our energy trying to prove our value to others is because we have believed the lie of our own worthlessness. The tragic irony is, despite all the good we may do to prove our worth to others, in the end, we only did it to prop up our broken false self.

This old or false self must be taken off, deconstructed, crucified, dead, and buried. This only happens when we dare to believe the gloriously beautiful truth about ourselves. We are created in the image of God. We are deeply known by God, and we are profoundly loved by God, and because God loves us, we are, in fact, lovable and worthy of love. This is true not because of anything we do or don't do or who we are or aren't, but because of who God is and what God has done. This is what it means that we "have clothed [our]selves with the new self, which is being renewed in knowledge according to the image of its creator" (v. 10 NRSV).

The knowledge we are being renewed in is this:

> The Spirit you received does not make you slaves, so that you live in fear again; rather, the Spirit you

received brought about your adoption to sonship. And by him we cry, "*Abba,* Father." (Rom. 8:15)

To repent means to renounce the lies of the old or false self and walk into one's new or true self. It happens as we believe and are renewed in the knowledge of God and the gospel, which is this: I am no longer a slave to fear. I am a child of God.

Domino #3|9 warrants a slogan of sorts: "If you fake it, you will never make it."

The Prayer

Abba Father, we thank you for your Son, Jesus, who is the image of the invisible God, the exact representation of your being. Thank you that I am created in his image. Reveal to me the lies I have believed about myself. Give me the courage to renounce them and the grace to run from them into the truth of who you are. I want to be renewed in knowledge in the image of my Creator. We pray in Jesus' name. Amen.

The Questions

- How do you relate to this notion of the old, false self and the new, true self?
- Are you aware of your false self? Yes Have you discovered how deep it goes and how difficult it is to root out? Yes, I have
- What do you think the next steps look like on this journey of being renewed in knowledge in the image of your Creator?

Continually observing if I am still on the right path, through prayer and meditation.

26 Gentile Lives Matter, but Not Why We Think

COLOSSIANS 3:11 NRSV | In that renewal there is no longer Greek and Jew, circumcised and uncircumcised, barbarian, Scythian, slave and free; but Christ is all and in all!

Consider This

Gentile lives matter. Barbarian lives matter. Slave lives matter.

Of course they do, but not why we think. What's interesting is, Paul doesn't choose this approach in his correspondence. He begins where he always begins, with Jesus, the image of the invisible God.

He does not start with historical realities, sociological categories, economic disparities, political concerns, or justice issues. He starts with theology. He begins with the kingdom of God. In the kingdom of God there are many distinctions between people, but there is no difference. Why? Because all are created in the image of God. In fact, it takes all of us to reflect the image of God. Only the image of God reflects such diverse distinctiveness while unifying it all in the same essence.

My growing conviction is, if we do not start with Jesus in these matters of our distinctiveness, we will never get to Jesus. Instead, we will allow our distinctiveness to devolve into differences that divide us. This is not naive idealism. "All men are created equal," is idealism. When Paul says, "there is no Gentile and Jew, circumcised and uncircumcised, barbarian, Scythian, slave and free; but Christ is all and is in all" (v. 11 NRSV), he is not espousing an ideal. He references the blood-bought redemption of a diabolically broken race, which can only be found in one place—Jesus Christ.

Because of the political currents, the zeitgeist of our age will not enter the conversation on these terms, so we wind up submitting to all things historical, sociological, economic, political, and judicial. We search for a creative ideal we will never find. All the while our Creator God offers the furthest thing from an ideal: the cross.

And what irony: the only one who would be all-inclusive— "but Christ is all and is in all"—is excluded on the grounds of his alleged exclusivity.

Theology rules. That's Domino #3|11.

The Prayer

Abba Father, we thank you for your Son, Jesus, who is our only hope for unity in diversity and community in the midst of chaos. Forgive me for how I have sought to create difference from distinctiveness. Reorder my own thinking about who matters and why. We pray in Jesus' name. Amen.

The Questions

- So, what if we began with Christ instead of all these other categories when it comes to all the ways we are divided in the present day?

- Why don't the followers of Jesus want to begin with theological concerns rather than get drawn first into all the other divisive and reactionary categories of our time?
- How does the cross challenge and defeat your idealism?

27 Why We Need to Practice Our Faith in Full Pads

COLOSSIANS 3:12–13 | Therefore, as God's chosen people, holy and dearly loved, clothe yourselves with compassion, kindness, humility, gentleness and patience. Bear with each other and forgive one another if any of you has a grievance against someone. Forgive as the Lord forgave you.

1 Or endure —meaning to suffer patiently

Consider This

Compassion. Kindness. Humility. Gentleness. Patience.

I have always thought of these as the goals or the outcomes of the life hid with Christ in God. I am beginning to understand them as the ways and means to get to the goals and outcomes. Because I understand life primarily through the lens of my individual-ness, I think of these things primarily as individual pursuits.

To be sure, Paul is talking about individual responsibility, but his endgame is not a bunch of isolated individuals trying to behave, living in towns, cities, and suburbs, and loosely connected through the building across town commonly referred to as the church.

Paul gives us the ground-game strategy for a changed world. It happens when a group of people do this:

> Clothe yourselves with compassion, kindness, humility, gentleness and patience. Bear with each other and forgive one another if any of you has a grievance against someone. Forgive as the Lord forgave you. (vv. 12b–13)

This is what Paul means by "church," the temple of the living God, the place where the Holy Spirit is pleased to dwell, and the home of miracles.

Compassion, kindness, humility, gentleness, and patience aren't virtues to which we must aspire. No, they are our uniform. Think of them as the pads a football player wears to play the game. Mustn't this be what Paul means when he says, "clothe yourselves"?

> Bear with each other and forgive one another if any of you has a grievance against someone. Forgive as the Lord forgave you. (v. 13)

Doesn't that feel like protective gear meant to preserve our fragile selves and relationships in the midst of a world where sin destroys us and causes us to destroy each other? Because we have died with Christ and are now raised with Christ, we have been given a new uniform. Before, these were just clothes in the window of a store we could never afford to enter. Now they are the uniforms in our very closets. Football players don't put on their pads because they feel like it. They put them on so they can play the game.

When we put on this gear and live out our lives together, we create the kind of community that changes the world. We become like a burning bush, on fire but not being consumed. People can't look away. In fact, the closer they get, the more they hear the voice of God whispering, "*Come closer. Holy ground! Take off your shoes.*"

Compassion, kindness, humility, gentleness, and patience create the conditions where the Holy Spirit heals wounded people, mends broken relationships, and reverses intractable situations. These are not things that I do, nor are they outcomes that we can accomplish together. These are the things only God can do, and these are the kinds of communities where he does them.

How shall we classify Domino #3|12? How about Full Pads.

The Prayer

Abba Father, we thank you for your Son, Jesus, who is the very embodiment of compassion, kindness, humility, gentleness, and patience. Thank you for not only the way he has forgiven us, but the ways he continues to bear with us. Show me what it means to put on these clothes in the power of the Spirit and help me to stop seeing them as impossible ways to manage my behavior. We pray in Jesus' name. Amen.

The Questions

- How do you understand the big idea (individual behavior management versus community mentality) I am trying to communicate today? Is it making sense?
- What do you make of the clothing (i.e., football pads) metaphor with respect to compassion, kindness, humility, gentleness, patience, and so forth?
- Have you ever been in a transformative community who put on compassion, kindness, humility, gentleness, and patience and who genuinely forgave and bore with one another? What happened? Valley Walk to Emmaus

The Problem with Good Morals

28

COLOSSIANS 3:14 | And over all these virtues put on love, which binds them all together in perfect unity.

Consider This

There is a word inserted in today's Scripture reading that can't be found in the original Greek text. See if you can spot it.

If you guessed *virtues*, you are correct. It happens from time to time. In order to make the meanings flow clearer in a given language, a translator will help it along. It's a perfectly legitimate thing to do, and it rarely changes the meaning. At times, though, it can have the effect of shading the interpretation by triggering in the reader a whole range of additional meanings that come from their own cultural context.

Virtue is such a word, and if the translators were translating an actual Greek word here, it would be less of a problem. They are not. Most translations leave it at "these," as in, "And over all these put on love, which binds them all together in perfect unity." "These," of course, refers to "compassion, kindness, humility, gentleness and patience," from verse 12.

So, what's the problem with "virtue"? The problem is the framework it sets up with its half brother, "vice." Virtue and vice shift the concept of holiness and sin from health versus sickness to honor versus shame. I don't think the unfolding vision of the Bible is to produce God-fearing moral citizens. Rather, the vision is to birth God-filled human beings: men, women, girls, and boys who embody a quality of holiness exuding from the very image of God, who is Jesus Christ.

The biblical word for this is not *virtue.* It is *love.* I am convinced the Bible calls us to leave behind all the old earth-bound categories of immoral and moral, vice and virtue, shame and honor, and even sinner and saint (in the limited ways we think of them). This is why the Bible does not set forth a moralistic behavior management approach, but rather a death-and-resurrection reality. The Bible concerns itself with the movement of the decisively supernatural reality of holy love into the decidedly human realm characterized by the sickness of sin and the domain of death.

Think about it: compassion, kindness, humility, gentleness, and patience, bound together in the perfect unity of love—these are not the ruts of morality but the realm of the miraculous. We don't need a moral vision. We need a vision of holiness—a.k.a. the love of God in Jesus Christ.

I'm willing to be wrong about this, but here's how I see it. Morality is a very low bar, and if that's what we are aiming for, our lives will hover back and forth just above and below this threshold. Virtue is simply good morals on steroids. Love, on the other hand, is the holy presence of Jesus Christ filling human beings together to the measure of all the fullness of God. This is the secret long hidden and now revealed. It's not about aspiring to better behavior but about becoming abandoned to Jesus.

> And over all these virtues put on love, which binds them all together in perfect unity. (v. 14)

No more moralizing. Domino #3|14 will remind us.

The Prayer

Abba Father, we thank you for your Son, Jesus, who not only embodies the holiness of love, but imparts it to us. Come, Holy Spirit, and lift me out of the broken ways of virtue, vice, honor, and shame, and lead me into the resurrection life of love. I will never find it on my own. We pray in Jesus' name. Amen.

The Questions

- These are massive thoughts I can hardly get my mind around. How are you thinking about them?
- Do you tend to agree or disagree with this contrast between virtue and holy love? Does it make any difference in your daily life?
- What are the implications for you of getting life out of moral categories of virtue and vice and into the realm of death and resurrection?

29 | What on Earth Is the Peace of Christ?

COLOSSIANS 3:15 | Let the peace of Christ rule in your hearts, since as members of one body you were called to peace. And be thankful.

Consider This

Question for you: What is the "peace of Christ"? What on earth does this mean? Like many of you, I've been in a lot of church services where people walk around saying, "Peace," to one another and shaking hands. Surely that can't be it! It's another one of those motions disconnected from the movement. Is the peace of Christ a feeling or a mood or a soft sentiment, or is it something more firm and tangible?

On the night before Jesus gave himself up for us, he said this to his disciples:

> "Peace I leave with you; my peace I give you. I do not give to you as the world gives. Do not let your hearts be troubled and do not be afraid." (John 14:27)

We hear a lot these days about "peace through strength." I think they heard it a lot back in those days too. It was called the *Pax Romana*—the Peace of Rome. The peace of Christ was something altogether different.

The lordship of Caesar guaranteed the Peace of Rome through the strength of military might. The lordship of Jesus stood in direct contrast, a crucified king raised from the dead. The peace of Christ is an unshakable peace that comes through apparent weakness, won through death and resurrection. It is the bond formed in a group of people who have given up on the kingdoms of this world and taken up the way of the cross. The peace of Christ is the peace of the cross, a place of unbridled chaos and unutterable pain intersected with the complete reverse of resurrection.

Peace through weakness. It's what a lot of us need right now, because our strength has failed. We need to lean into a community of peace; people who get the mysterious reality of death and resurrection because they have lived through it. We need the kind of peace the world can't give us. We need the peace of Christ. We don't need someone speaking mindless religious words to us. We need someone to embrace us, chaos and all, and not let go when the embrace is over.

The peace of Christ be with you.
And also with you.

It had better be more than that, church.

> Let the peace of Christ rule in your hearts, since as members of one body you were called to peace. And be thankful.

Real Peace. Domino #3|15 will be our sign.

The Prayer

Abba Father, we thank you for your Son, Jesus, who is our peace. In the midst of the complex chaos that swirls in my life, where solutions are nonexistent, I desperately need the peace of Jesus. I need this peace to rule in my heart. Come, Holy Spirit, and fill me with this peace, and make me a bearer of it to others. We pray in Jesus' name. Amen.

The Questions

- Have you ever wondered what the peace of Christ is? How do you describe it?
- Is your heart troubled by the chaos swarming around you? What would peace look and feel like to you?
- What does your synthetic or artificial or counterfeit peace look like? What do you turn to instead of the peace of Christ?

Why the Songs May Matter More than the Sermon

30

COLOSSIANS 3:16 | Let the message of Christ dwell among you richly as you teach and admonish one another with all wisdom through psalms, hymns, and songs from the Spirit, singing to God with gratitude in your hearts.

Consider This

Have you ever thought of singing songs to God as a way of teaching and admonishing one another with the message of Christ? I haven't either.

We pretty much think of teaching and admonishing as coming from one person who stands in the front of a room, delivering a message to a group of people who listen.

As I reflect on today's text about letting "the message of Christ dwell among you richly as you teach and admonish one another with all wisdom through psalms, hymns, and songs from the Spirit, singing to God with gratitude in your hearts," I can't help but think of the church of my childhood. I grew up in a small church in rural Arkansas. We were there every Sunday, and I have the Perfect Attendance pins to prove it. When I get still and listen, I can still hear the singing . . .

On a hill far away stood an old rugged cross, the emblem of suffering of shame. And I love that old cross, where the dearest and best for a world of lost sinners was slain . . .

A mighty fortress is our God, a bulwark never failing; our helper he amidst the flood of mortal ills prevailing . . .

'Tis so sweet to trust in Jesus, just to take him at his word; just to rest upon his promise; just to know thus saith the Lord . . .

When we walk with the Lord, in the light of his Word, what a glory he sheds on our way! While we do his good will, he abides with us still, and with all who will trust and obey.

Love divine, all love's excelling, joy of heav'n to earth come down, fix in us thy humble dwelling, all thy faithful mercies crown. Jesus thou art all compassion, pure unbounded love thou art, visit us with thy salvation, enter every trembling heart.[2]

"Let the message of Christ dwell among you richly as you teach and admonish one another with all wisdom through psalms, hymns, and songs from the Spirit, singing to God with gratitude in your hearts" (v. 16). I never imagined that while we were singing to God we were teaching and admonishing one another, but when I think about it now, that's exactly

---

2   George Bennard, "The Old Rugged Cross," (public domain); Martin Luther, "A Mighty Fortress Is Our God," (public domain); Louisa M. R. Stead, "'Tis so Sweet to Trust in Jesus," (public domain); John H. Sammis, "When We Walk with the Lord," (public domain); and Charles Wesley, "Beecher," (public domain).

what happened. The singing wasn't particularly good, but the message of Christ was undeniable. I can still hear Peepaw's voice singing out above the crowd, loud, proud, and slightly off-key. I could pick my parents' voices out of the choir. My best friend, Jeff, sat a few rows back. Though he couldn't carry a tune in a bucket, he added his voice to the cacophony of teachers anyway. At the time it seemed pretty ordinary. I see it now as a glorious treasure, extraordinary richness.

> So I'll cherish the old rugged cross, till my trophies at last I lay down.
> I will cling to the old rugged cross, and exchange it someday for a crown.

Though I know they mattered, I can't remember a single sermon. I can't forget the songs. Same for you? We may be onto something here . . . but what?

> Let the message of Christ dwell among you richly as you teach and admonish one another with all wisdom through psalms, hymns, and songs from the Spirit, singing to God with gratitude in your hearts. (v. 16)

Never Stop Singing. Write it on the blank side of Domino #3|16.

The Prayer

Abba Father, we thank you for your Son, Jesus, who is our story and our song. He is the message and the melody. Awaken me to my singing voice, even if I can't sing, because it's not about the singing but the song. We pray in Jesus' name. Amen.

The Questions

- What songs come to mind in your memory?
- What is it about songs and singing that teach us at another level than speaking and sermons?
- What about this dynamic of a group of people teaching and admonishing each other in this way? Ever considered that?

31 On Method Acting and the Call of Discipleship

COLOSSIANS 3:17 NRSV | And whatever you do, in word or deed, do everything in the name of the Lord Jesus, giving thanks to God the Father through him.

Consider This

Have you ever heard of method acting? Method actors enter into their characters at the beginning of a play or movie-making process, and they never leave characters until the whole project is done.

Daniel Day-Lewis is famous for his method acting skills. When he takes on the character of Abraham Lincoln, he becomes Abraham Lincoln. On the set and off, he will answer to no other name. He speaks of "the gravitational pull of another life that sparks one's curiosity."[3]

For my money, today's text calls us to a form of method acting: "And whatever you do, in word or deed, do everything in the name of the Lord Jesus, giving thanks to God the Father through him" (Col. 3:17 NRSV).

"Whatever you do" knows no limitation. It is totalizing and comprehensive. Paul instructs that we are to never leave character. And the character is Jesus Christ. Doesn't this verse complete the trajectory of how the chapter began?

> Since, then, you have been raised with Christ, set your hearts on things above, where Christ is, seated at the right hand of God. Set your minds on things above, not on earthly things. For you died, and your life is now hidden with Christ in God. (Col. 3:1–3)

If I'm honest, and you know I aspire to be, I have mostly read this verse as I would read a sentimental refrigerator magnet, with an internal response like, "Sure, of course I'll try to do that." I basically filed it in the same place I have put so many other lofty Bible verses—biblical self-improvement, you know—try harder to be a better Christian.

The force of the whole chapter, if not the whole New Testament, is not "try harder to do better and be a better

---

3   Geoffrey Macnab, "The Madness of Daniel Day-Lewis—a Unique Method that Has Led to a Deserved Third Oscar," *Independent* (UK), February 25, 2013, http://www.independent.co.uk/arts-entertainment/films/features/the-madness-of-daniel-day-lewis-a-unique-method-that-has-led-to-a-deserved-third-oscar-8510704.html.

Christian." The message of the gospel is to give up on that whole project; that former, false self is dead. Arise into the new creation of your raised-from-the-dead life. Our good-to-great mentality must die. The "hidden with Christ in God" reality must rise.

You and I are method actors, only this is not a movie. It our life. We never leave character. In those moments when I do, I want people to say something like, "John David was really out of character yesterday."

Let's help each other with this. The Holy Spirit is ever willing to do this in us, but he works best in the midst of a few people banded together to see it through in each other's lives. That's the way those early Methodists took the world by storm. See what I just did there? Method-ists. They banded together as method actors. It's an idea whose time has come again.

Let's name Domino #3|17 The Method Actor.

The Prayer

Abba Father, we thank you for your Son, Jesus, who is our character and our method. Thank you for the way he can make me to be most truly myself when he trains my character to be like his. Come, Holy Spirit, and take me deep into the character of Christ so much that I never leave. In Jesus' name, amen.

The Questions

- How do you relate to this notion of method acting?

- Have you typically thought of Colossians 3:17 as an aspirational thought but little else? How does today's daily text change this?
- Do you have a few people gathered around you to help you delve deeper into the character and to stay in character all the time—every thought, word, and deed?

Why Women Won't Submit to Men, and Vice Versa

32

COLOSSIANS 3:18–19 | Wives, submit yourselves to your husbands, as is fitting in the Lord. Husbands, love your wives and do not be harsh with them.

Consider This

Submission. It's a word we love to hate. It evokes images of a mixed martial arts cage fight. Submission must be the worst possible way to lose. It happens when one fighter is held down so oppressively and inescapably by another fighter that he taps out, which means he taps on the mat with his hand to signify his submission, and the referee stops the fight. I think I would rather be knocked out than forced to submit like this.

Is it any wonder so many women have an almost allergic reaction to texts like today's: "Wives, submit yourselves to your husbands, as is fitting in the Lord" (v. 18)? Submission carries connotations of being overpowered and dominated. Wives, allow yourselves to be overpowered and dominated by your husbands—just tap out. Surely this can't be what Paul means.

Here's my theory on the case. Paul is proposing a very radical thing here. In the old framework, under the curse going all the way back to Eden, wives would have had no choice but to be subject to their husbands: "Your desire will be for your husband, and he will rule over you" (Gen. 3:16b). You will remember a few verses back where Paul said, "Here there is no Gentile or Jew, circumcised or uncircumcised, barbarian, Scythian, slave or free, but Christ is all, and is in all" (Col. 3:11). He might as easily have added here the same pairing he inserted as he expressed this point to the Galatians: "neither male nor female" (Gal. 3:28 KJV).

The new creation is "in Christ," and it is now. Everything has changed. Husbands no longer rule over wives. Submission as imagined by the curse is out. Submission as imagined by the gospel is in. Hear Paul again, and particularly the six-word addendum at the end: "Wives, submit yourselves to your husbands, as is fitting in the Lord" (Col. 3:18).

In the new creation, wives do not live under the curse of being ruled by their husbands. Paul is asking them to step outside the old power paradigm and into the ethos of the kingdom of God. In this all-too-rarified realm, submission means voluntary surrender, not to one's husband, but to Jesus; not giving up one's rights, but laying them down in preference for others. In short, submission means having the same mind in you that was in Christ Jesus (see Philippians 2:5) and all that this entails.

To be clear, it would never be "fitting in the Lord" for a wife to submit to a husband who seeks to rule over her, violate her sense of personhood, or act in any way that might remotely resemble abuse.

Paul is actually saying something very radical here. Submission to one's husband is now the prerogative, the free choice of the wife, taking submission out of the structures of power and into the realm of holy love. I am sure I will ruffle some feathers with this, but why do we set our sights on equal rights? Isn't that far too low a bar for God's people? We are following the One "Who, being in very nature God, did not consider equality with God something to be used to his own advantage" (or "grasped" in the ESV; Phil. 2:6). Submission presupposes no obligation; only freedom.

"Husbands, love your wives and do not be harsh with them" (Col. 3:19). It's another way of saying, "Husbands, you are not the ruler of your wives. You are not their lord. In fact, in the new creation, everything is reversed. You are just the opposite—their humble servant. You are not surrendering some of your power to them so they can be somehow equal to you. No, you are surrendering all of your power to Jesus alone, who will empower you by the Holy Spirit to become the servant of your wife. After all, he refers to his people, the church, as his bride.

The kingdom comes in response to radical surrender to Jesus, "in heaven," which is manifest through radical submission to each other, "on earth." Remember how the chapter began, "set your hearts on things above, where Christ is, seated at the right hand of God" (v. 1).

We must take care not to baptize our American idealism with Christian theology. While the latter has certainly informed the former, they are decisively different visions. We don't need better ideas, ideals, and ideologies. We need better theology.

The handle for Domino #3|18 and #3|19 is simple: Submission.

The Prayer

Abba Father, we thank you for your Son, Jesus, who, far from an idea, is the Word of God made human flesh. Forgive us for the ways we want to press him into the service of our ideals and ideologies. Come, Holy Spirit, and lift my heart and mind and eyes to the heavenly vision of the very real kingdom of God. I'm ready to renounce every other vision. We pray in Jesus' name. Amen.

The Questions

- How does this challenge your views of what submission means?
- How do you understand the whole concept of one's rights and how they should be exercised in light of the cross of Jesus Christ?

- What is it about you that causes you to resist humbling yourself as a woman? As a man? As a wife (if you are married)? As a husband? What are you afraid of?

What Parents Must Understand about Parenting

33

COLOSSIANS 3:20–21 NRSV | Children, obey your parents in everything, for this is your acceptable duty in the Lord. Fathers, do not provoke your children, or they may lose heart.

Consider This

All Scripture memory systems for children naturally begin with Colossians 3:20. It is no surprise that Paul would exhort children to, "obey your parents in everything." Of course children must obey their parents.

The stunner is Paul's word to fathers. "Fathers, do not provoke your children, or they may lose heart" (v. 21). In the first century, no one tended to care too much about children becoming discouraged by their fathers.

Why did Paul care about children? Because Jesus cared about children. Jesus cares about children because God cares about children.

> Then people brought little children to Jesus for him to place his hands on them and pray for them. But the disciples rebuked them.
>
> Jesus said, "Let the little children come to me, and do not hinder them, for the kingdom of heaven belongs to such as these." When he had placed his hands on them, he went on from there. (Matt. 19:13–15)

Children form their primary image of who God is through the way they are parented. If a parent is harsh, they will naturally, albeit unknowingly, assume God is harsh. If a parent is filled with compassion, kindness, humility, gentleness, and patience, the children will unknowingly assume this is what God is like. This makes parenting all at once the most practical and the most theological task in the world.

Here's the bottom line for those of us who are presently parenting children: we can fool a lot of people a lot of the time, but we can't fool our children. Whatever is in me will come out in my parenting. The surest way for my children to have a true sense of who the real God is and what the real God is like is for me to be a real Christian. Hence, my chief responsibility as a Christian parent is to be a real Christian. And the only way I can be a real Christian is to be filled with all the fullness of God.

Domino #3|20 is Home Training.

The Prayer

Abba Father, we thank you for your Son, Jesus, in whom all your fullness is pleased to dwell. Thank you that we have been given fullness in him. Come, Holy Spirit, and awaken me to the reality of being filled with all the fullness of God, especially for the sake of all of our children. We pray in Jesus' name. Amen.

The Questions

- Have you ever thought of parenting as a theological task? How did the way you were parented impact your image of God?
- Have you given consideration to what it means to parent "in Christ"?
- Remember: the secret is not in your parenting skills; the secret is "Christ in you." This means grace-based parenting—grace for our children and also grace for ourselves when we stumble. How about that?

Should Slaves Obey Their Masters?

34

COLOSSIANS 3:22–4:1 NRSV | Slaves, obey your earthly masters in everything, not only while being watched and in order to please them, but wholeheartedly, fearing the Lord.

Whatever your task, put yourselves into it, as done for the Lord and not for your masters, since you know that from the Lord you will receive the inheritance as your reward; you serve the Lord Christ. For the wrongdoer will be paid back for whatever wrong has been done, and there is no partiality. Masters, treat your slaves justly and fairly, for you know that you also have a Master in heaven.

Consider This

Slaves, obey your earthly masters in everything. (v. 22a)

Surely this must be among the most controversial texts in all of Scripture. Suppose a child living in a remote part of the world reads (or has read to them) Colossians 3 today. Suppose that child was a modern-day slave making mud bricks or grinding grain. We would want that child to heed verse 20, about obeying his or her parents, right? But how would we expect that child to deal with today's text? How would we have expected slaves in America in the nineteenth century to deal with it?

Just a few pages earlier, with the stroke of a pen, Paul seemed to abolish slavery when he said "In Christ there is neither slave nor free" (Gal. 3:28, paraphrased). Now he says, "Slaves, obey your masters." We need to go all the way back to verse 2 to frame our understanding:

To God's holy people in Colossae, the faithful brothers and sisters in Christ . . . (Col. 1:2a)

Remember those four key words, "In Colossae . . . in Christ"? It is only as the "in Christ" reality takes root "in Colossae" that the new creation begins to flourish and change. So, Paul begins with the new reality, and then he goes to work in the real world. You can't expect to read the letter on Sunday and abolish slavery on Monday; however, everyone who heard the letter can change the nature of slavery immediately through the power of the Holy Spirit changing their own hearts.

On the one hand, change cannot wait on new laws to be formed. The kind of change most needed cannot even be effected by laws. It must happen in the hearts and minds of masters and slaves. On the other hand, slaves can't wait on masters to change (i.e., come to Jesus). Gradualism, as Martin Luther King Jr. called it, is not a strategy. We can look to the likes of Harriet Tubman and Sojourner Truth on the one hand and William Wilberforce on the other to see the ways salvation "in Christ" upends sin "in England" and "in America" through the abolition of slavery.

As you are likely aware, slavery in the world today is worse than it has ever been. There are many modern-day Tubmans and Truths and Wilberforces striking major blows on a daily basis. I would encourage us all to join them in one way or another as a part of our discipleship to Jesus.

"Slaves, obey your earthly masters in everything" (v. 22a). Paul is not somehow affirming the institution of slavery in the Bible. He is dealing with discipleship on Monday morning in Colossae. On another front, Paul is working on behalf of one of his associate pastors, Onesimus, who happens to be a runaway slave. That's what his letter to Philemon, also in the New Testament, is all about—setting slaves free.

No Longer Slaves. It's a good moniker for Domino #3|22.

The Prayer

Abba Father, we thank you for your Son, Jesus, who being in very nature God took on the nature of a slave. Open my eyes to the ways I am yet enslaved to sin, and help me understand how my own slavery contributes to slavery everywhere it is found. I want to live fully "in Christ," and I want that for everyone else. We pray in Jesus' name. Amen.

The Questions

- How do you reflect on the reality that the Bible has been used to justify slavery through the centuries owing to texts like today's?
- How do you deal with the fact that sweeping social change takes time and yet an approach of gradualism is not an acceptable strategy?
- Are you presently involved in the movement to end slavery in the world? Check out enditmovement.com to learn more.

From Playing Dominoes to the Domino Effect

35

COLOSSIANS 4:2 | Devote yourselves to prayer, being watchful and thankful.

Consider This

Throughout this study series I have likened particular verses to dominoes. Does #2|2 or #3|3 ring a bell? Let's remember again the secret of the domino effect. A two-inch-tall domino can tip into and topple a four-and-a-half-inch-tall domino and a four-and-a-half-inch tall domino can topple a domino just over a foot tall, and that one can fell a domino at two-and-a-half-feet tall. Here's the domino effect. When you get to the twenty-third domino in this progression, you've just toppled the Eiffel Tower. When you come to the thirty-first domino, you just knocked over something three thousand feet higher than Mount Everest. As I said at the beginning of this book, sit down for this next one. At domino number fifty-seven, you are approaching the moon.

Devote yourselves to prayer, being watchful and thankful. (v. 2)

This text is the antidote to casual prayer. The Greek term behind what often feels like the perfectly innocuous word "devote," is *proskartereo.* Let's say that together: *pros-car-ter-eh-o*. It means a fanatically fixated focus. The old word for this kind of prayer was "travailing prayer." It's a word we are working to bring back into fashion with the New Room movement (of which I so badly want all of you to be a part). Travailing, or fanatically fixated, focused prayer, cannot be limited to a single domino. It's the DNA of every one of these dominoes. It's what gives the dominoes their innate tipping power.

We see this amazing domino effect most prominently and profoundly in the book of Acts. This whole idea of *proskartereo* figures prominently in each of the following passages. See if you can spot it.

> They all joined together constantly in prayer, along with the women and Mary the mother of Jesus, and with his brothers. (Acts 1:14)

> They devoted themselves to the apostles' teaching and to fellowship, to the breaking of bread and to prayer. (Acts 2:42)

> Every day they continued to meet together in the temple courts. They broke bread in their homes and ate together with glad and sincere hearts. (Acts 2:46)

> "Brothers and sisters, choose seven men from among you who are known to be full of the Spirit and wisdom. We will turn this responsibility over to them and will give our attention to prayer and the ministry of the word." (Acts 6:3–4)

Remember, the dominoes tipped from the Upper Room with 120 people to the day of Pentecost with 3,000, and all the way to the present day and some 2 billion Christians around the world. In domino effect terms we've been to the moon and back a thousand times, and the dominoes are still falling. Impossible things keep happening. And again, great awakenings are still on the horizon.

We need to wrap our minds and hearts around these things. Sometimes I think our churches are just playing dominoes when we could be playing with the domino effect. We don't want to look back at the end of our days and realize we were just playing dominoes.

Domino #4|2 will be code named *Proskartereo*, alias The Travailer.

The Prayer

Abba Father, we thank you for your Son, Jesus, who is both the cause and the effect of the kingdom of God and the church against which the gates of hell will never prevail. Come, Holy Spirit! Teach and train me for this way of *proskartereo*. I confess I am incapable of it apart from you. We pray in Jesus' name. Amen.

The Questions

- What do you think about this idea of the domino effect and the implications for our faith in the world today?

We need to always be excited for and ready for the next effect in the faith. Patiently and prayerfully fixated and focused.

111

- On a scale of 1 to 10, with 1 being casual and 10 being travailing, where would you rate your prayer life? *10, will the time almost const* (handwritten)
- What simple step might you take to advance one number higher on the scale? *Seminary lol.* (handwritten) *to pray openly with others in public* (handwritten)

Honestly to pray openly with others in public if there is a need. (handwritten)

36

Why I Sometimes Want to Cuss for the Glory of God—but I Don't!

COLOSSIANS 4:3–4 | And pray for us, too, that God may open a door for our message, so that we may proclaim the mystery of Christ, for which I am in chains. Pray that I may proclaim it clearly, as I should.

Consider This

Hang on! Did he just say chains? Why are we just now hearing about this? All of this magisterial manifesto on the mystery of Christ, and only in the last chapter does he tell us he is in prison! This is one of those places where I want to artfully arrange a string of cuss words together for dramatic effect . . . but I won't.

Go back and read it through again. You won't find the first word of his unholy accommodations until Domino #4|3. That's amazing, Paul! And all this time we thought this masterpiece of a letter was flowing out of your morning quiet times from some scenic vista on the Mediterranean Sea.

I think this is hilarious (handwritten)

> And pray for us, too, that God may open a door for our message, so that we may proclaim the mystery of Christ, for which I am in chains. (v. 3)

Here's the kicker. When Paul asks for prayer for God to open a door for his message, he's not talking about the door of the prison. He's not talking about a door for himself at all. He's talking first and foremost about a door "for our message," a.k.a. the gospel of Jesus Christ. Note also his use of the plural, "we." Gospel proclamation is a team sport; think football, not golf. This is not pray for "Paul of Tarsus Apostolic Holy Ghost Ministries dot-com." Paul has been benched, taken out of the game, sidelined, locked down, and yes, even chained up. Do you have any ideas how many doors have opened between Paul's imprisoned pen and today's reading for this message of the mystery of Christ to reach us? Talk about the domino effect!

And that right there, my friends, is the mystery of Christ. The message of the gospel can't be reduced to messaging. That's the mistake we make. The message of the gospel is a mystery. In the worst, darkest, most apparently unfruitful and least-fulfilling moment of Paul's life, he's proclaiming the mystery of Christ. And isn't that the mystery itself—that the apostle Paul, en route to his own cross, can't stop declaring the wonders of Jesus?

"In Christ" is not a theory for Paul. It's not a morning devotion. It is his life. The mystery is that the further Paul plunges into the grip of death, the higher he rises in the power of the resurrection. I honestly think Paul got so carried away with

Jesus in this letter, he forgot for a minute he was in prison. That's the mystery of Christ: death and resurrection!

That's what I want for you and for me. So many of us are in chains at the moment, of one sort or another. We are tied up by our circumstances or tied down by our problems. We or those we love are facing intractable difficulties. Others of us have become ensnared in sin that will not let go. In fact, many of us are beyond bailing out. It's time to move beyond Jesus sprinkles, singing songs in church, and putting a tip in the offering plate. It's time for wholesale abandonment to Jesus—to the mystery of Christ. We must have death and resurrection—not in theory, but in fact.

Again, it makes me want to cuss for the glory of God. But I won't!

Let's call Domino #4|3 The Door Opener.

The Prayer

Abba Father, we thank you for your Son, Jesus, who went to prison with Paul and, by the cross, transformed a prison into the witness of the power of the gospel. Do that in my life. Take the mess of my life and of this world and make of it a street-level sanctuary of the holy mystery of Christ, for my good and your glory. We pray in Jesus' name. Amen.

The Questions

- Did you realize Paul was in prison while he was writing Colossians? How does that impact your reading of it?

Yes, I knew about halfway into the book lol. I don't see it as a strike against him, but as a powerful testament $ witness.

- Are you, or is someone you know, facing an intractable imprisoning situation? How will today's text help you encourage yourself or the other person? How will you pray for the situation?
- Why is it that the hardest times produce the deepest witness of the mystery of Christ?

The Everyday Ministry of Passing the Salt

37

COLOSSIANS 4:5–6 | Be wise in the way you act toward outsiders; make the most of every opportunity. <u>Let your conversation</u> be always full of grace, seasoned with salt, so that you may know how to answer everyone.

Consider This

When I was a young teenager, I had the good fortune of discovering a treasure trove of a book on my parents' bookshelf. I'm not exactly certain why I pulled it off the shelf, and even less certain of why I read it, but of the fact that it changed my life I could not be more certain. The author of the book was Dale Carnegie, and you have already likely guessed the title, *How to Win Friends and Influence People*.

I remember a lot about the book, though one lesson stands out and towers above the rest: "Become genuinely interested in other people." It's what I hear when I read today's text:

Be wise in the way you act toward outsiders. (v. 5a)

By "be wise" Paul doesn't mean "be on your guard." No, he means, let your guard down. He means, don't be about yourself. Be about them. It begins with Carnegie's rule: "Become genuinely interested in other people." Why? Beyond the first step of noticing people, becoming genuinely interested in them, is the posture of love. It lets them know they are, in fact, interesting.

Make the most of every opportunity. (v. 5b)

What is the opportunity? I used to think the opportunity was to try and work in some way to share the gospel message with them, which in retrospect looks more like trying to get people enlisted on my multilevel marketing discipleship pyramid scheme.

I think of sharing the gospel differently now. It's more about the mystery than the messaging. As we have discussed, the message of the gospel is the mystery of Christ, and the mystery of Christ is Christ in us. To the extent I am attuned to "Christ in me," I can be present to the person sitting across from me. To the extent I can be present to that person, Christ will presence himself with us and the mystery will become manifest. As I become genuinely interested in another person, Jesus manifests his interest in him or her.

The opportunities are everywhere. The overwhelming majority of people in the world, outsiders or not, are not listened to. No one leans into them and listens with genuine interest. This is what supernatural love looks like in ordinary clothes.

> Let your conversation be always full of grace, seasoned with salt, so that you may know how to answer everyone. (v. 6)

I think of becoming genuinely interested in other people as salting a conversation. It brings out the flavor in them. It necessarily means becoming less interested in myself (a.k.a. less self-interested). What is it about salt that makes food so much more satisfying? Maybe we need to think more about passing the salt as it relates to what is on their plates and not so much about our own.

Let's call Domino #4|6 The Salt Shaker. It's another small one with exponential impact potential, and it can be tipped almost any way at any time.

The Prayer

Abba Father, we thank you for your Son, Jesus, who is the salt of the earth and who would so fill us with himself that we might become the same. Fill me with the fullness of Christ in my bearing toward others that I might become genuinely interested in them and that my interest could become an act of your love. We pray in Jesus' name. Amen.

The Questions

- When was the last time you experienced another person becoming genuinely interested in you? It can be rare.

Not sure, a co-worker perhaps,

117

- When was the last time you were intentional about becoming genuinely interested in another person whom you didn't know? *Recently at work*
- Why is this so rare in the world? How will you change this today? Tomorrow? *For we are in a fallen world,*

38 The Difference between Gospel Acclaim and Being Famous for the Gospel

COLOSSIANS 4:7–9 NRSV | Tychicus will tell you all the news about me; he is a beloved brother, a faithful minister, and a fellow servant in the Lord. I have sent him to you for this very purpose, so that you may know how we are and that he may encourage your hearts; he is coming with Onesimus, the faithful and beloved brother, who is one of you. They will tell you about everything here.

Consider This

Have you heard of Tychicus?

I've always thought of these closing greetings in Paul's letters as the honorable mentions section. Honestly, I've paid little to no attention to the names. It's always felt to me as though Paul was giving props to his posse or a shout-out to his entourage. I guess it's cool if you were Tychicus's uncle or something. Honorable mention in the Bible is no small thing.

Let me tell you a little bit about Tychicus. It turns out he was a rock star in his own right. We have it on good evidence that Tychicus was one of "the Seventy,"[4] the group of disciples Jesus sent out in Luke 10. Yes, Tychicus knew *the* Jesus. He was a direct disciple. He could have made a career out of that social capital, only there were no ministry careers in those days. So, he went to jail with Paul and carried his mail and whatever else needed to be done to push the movement forward. Though he was not famous for the gospel, nor ever shall he be, he was a person of gospel acclaim.

There's gospel acclaim and then there's being famous for the gospel. People who are famous for the gospel are a dime a dozen. No one's name gets mentioned in the New Testament because he or she wrote a viral blog post or authored a best-selling book or pastored a megachurch.

We live in the Kardashian age of marketing machines, where people become famous for simply being famous. It's not limited to Hollywood reality TV. The ministry is rife with fame hounds. We clickbait our way to a viral blog post. We write books and become YouTube stars. We are famous for the gospel without any real gospel acclaim. We haven't been in jail with the apostle Paul or been beaten within an inch of our life for our faith or otherwise buried our lives like seeds in some forgotten ghetto in Memphis.

---

4   NRSV and KJV: seventy; ESV and NIV: seventy-two.

In the scheme of things, very few people will ever be famous for the gospel. It's unfortunate how in the present age those are the people who get all the press and they tend to be the people we look to. The beauty of the gospel is that anyone can receive gospel acclaim—which means literally "to shout." Gospel acclaim is the shout of heaven, and it happens every time someone reckons with Domino #3|3—"For you died, and your life is now hidden with Christ in God" (Col. 3:3)—and tips Domino #3|1—"Since, then, you have been raised with Christ, set your hearts on things above, where Christ is, seated at the right hand of God" (Col. 3:1).

These days, the church would be better served if we knew a lot more names like Tychicus. We need to make it our business to find out the name of someone who was martyred last week, the young woman's name who left for Tanzania after college to translate the Bible into a language yet to be written down, the name of the farmer who loaned too much money to his workers without expectation of repayment, and the name of the woman who works at the corner coffee shop and quietly serves people more like a shepherd than a barista.

Let's call Domino #4|7 Tychicus, one who is small in stature but with massive tipping effect.

The Prayer

Abba Father, we thank you for your Son, Jesus, who is the gospel's acclaim. Train us to follow him and all those he acclaims. Save me from the seduction of seeking fame, and steer me clear of following the merely famous. We pray in Jesus' name. Amen.

The Questions

- Who comes to your mind when you think of a person of gospel acclaim? From the past? From the present?
- What is it about fame that is so seductive to our present age?
- What would it look like for you to set your sights on the hidden glory of gospel acclaim—to hear the shout of heaven?

On Volunteering for Prison

39

COLOSSIANS 4:10–11 ESV | Aristarchus my fellow prisoner greets you, and Mark the cousin of Barnabas (concerning whom you have received instructions—if he comes to you, welcome him), and Jesus who is called Justus. These are the only men of the circumcision among my fellow workers for the kingdom of God, and they have been a comfort to me.

Consider This

It's one thing to be locked up in prison against your will. It's quite another to volunteer. That's the story of Aristarchus. There are friends and then there are friends. Aristarchus wasn't some cool freedom fighter Paul met and befriended in prison. We have it on good evidence that Aristarchus and Epaphras alternated shifts of imprisonment back and forth between them so they could be alongside Paul to help support and care for his needs.

It's one thing to visit people who are in prison, and a good thing. It is love at a level of pure Jesus to become a prisoner in order to serve the imprisoned. Aristarchus and Epaphras checked their freedom at the door, fully entering into the vile, intolerable conditions of a Roman prison for the sake of the love of God. They became the prisoners of holy love.

Can I be honest about something? I've never done this. I've never done anything remotely close to this. Aristarchus and Epaphras challenge me to the core of my being. Their story challenges me to think about those people in my life who are in some kind of inescapable confinement of some sort. I find it easy to steer clear of situations that I can't somehow solve, choosing to spend my helpful energies in those scenarios where "a little help from my friends" will do the trick. I think Jesus wants me to be more involved with more unsolvable problems, in places where I have nothing to offer but his love through my 100-percent "with-them-ness." Isn't this exactly what Jesus has done with us?

I have disclosed to you before the nature of the trials I have faced in recent years and continue to face in my personal life. As I reflect on it, I have known Aristarchus and Epaphras through what continues to be the hardest season I have ever faced. Far beyond paying me a friendly visit, they have entered into my imprisonment with me. They have attended to my needs. As I think about it, they have effectively shackled themselves to me in a very "come what may" way. I can't, in words, express to you what that has meant. To say I am thankful does not begin to touch the levels of my gratitude.

It makes me want to become more of an Aristarchus and Epaphras in the lives of other people; people whose problem I can't solve and yet people who have needs for help and encouragement and the love of Jesus with skin on.

You too? *Let's all strive for friends like this, and*

A good descriptor for Domino #4|10: Cell Mates. *to be friends like this.*

The Prayer

Abba Father, we thank you for your Son, Jesus, who entered and enters our world and our lives so fully that he will never leave us. Come, Holy Spirit, and teach me this way of the cross, that resurrection only comes to those who willingly lay down their lives for others. Though so much in me resists, I want the mind of Christ. We pray in Jesus' name. Amen.

The Questions

- Have you encountered modern-day Aristarchus and Epaphras types in your life? What was that like?
- Have you been an Aristarchus and Epaphras type in the lives of others? What was that like?

• How are you challenged when it comes to entering into situations and challenges you can't solve or fix? What does the love of Jesus challenge you to do in those scenarios?

It challenges me to think of a way in my faith were I can sacrifice my time like Paul's Friends.

40 Why We Must Band Together or Fall Apart

COLOSSIANS 4:12–13 ESV | Epaphras, who is one of you, a servant of Christ Jesus, greets you, always struggling on your behalf in his prayers, that you may stand mature and fully assured in all the will of God. For I bear him witness that he has worked hard for you and for those in Laodicea and in Hierapolis.

Consider This

I'm seeing it today for the first time. Paul is in a band. Not a band as in Aerosmith or The Beatles, but a band of a few people who have allied themselves with Jesus to advance his purposes in the world. They are helping one another to mature in their faith and character; to become the kind of disciples they aspire to make of others; those who "stand mature and fully assured in all the will of God" (v. 12 ESV).

It's a prison band. We have been talking about them over the past few days—Tychicus, Aristarchus, John Mark, Epaphras, Luke, and Demas.

You've heard of infamous gangsters running organized crime rings from prison. Well, Paul and his band are running the kingdom of Jesus from prison. They are "in Christ," and "in chains," and the more in chains they are, the more in Christ they become. That's what happens in a band. This is how the power of the gospel works best—banded together.

Can't you see the map they're etching into the stone wall of the cell? There's Laodicea and Hierapolis, Ephesus, Colossae and Philippi, Thessalonica and Corinth. And they don't have any idea of France or England yet, or Arkansas!

Banding is about weaving a net through tying unbreakable knots forged by the love of God in human relationships. These knots become the nets that save the lives of countless others, rescuing them from drowning in the punishing seas of the world.

A band is not another domesticated small group filling a slot in the sociological structures of church belonging. A band is a missional outpost on the front lines of the war on darkness. Note how Paul describes the work of Epaphras in their band as, "always struggling on your behalf in his prayers" (v. 12b ESV). The Greek term there is _agonizomai,_ and it means something like "doing battle."

Are you ready to band together like this? A lot of people quietly dismiss this calling, thinking it's not something they need. Here's my question: What if it's not about you? What if it's about the world around you? What if it's your town or neighborhood or kids' schools or the heroin situation in your county that cries out for you to band together? Don't get me wrong. You need it for sure, whether you know it or now, but the world needs it even more. This is how the kingdom of God advances, not through singing songs in anonymous crowds on Sunday mornings, but through the unbreakable bonds of our prison bands as we link up arms and hearts and walk together into the captivity of the culture around us. This is how we sow for a great awakening.

My Daily Text dream is to sow a band in every county in America. This is why you like Seedbed and the Daily Text. It's not just another morning devotion. We are going somewhere together. We aren't servicing a domesticated church. No, we are resourcing an awakening movement. We are sowing for a great awakening. There's no time to waste.

Getting the band back together. That's how we will think of Domino #4|12.

The Prayer

Abba Father, we thank you for your Son, Jesus, who started the first band. Thank you for the way he is ever banding his disciples together to sow for a great awakening. Awaken me to this high and holy calling to band with a few for the sake of the many around me. We pray in Jesus' name. Amen.

The Questions

· Had you ever thought of Paul as working from the context of a band before? What do you think about it?

- Have you ever considered that starting a band might be as much for others as it is for you and your band?
- Are you open to joining the great band together to sow for a great awakening campaign? What hesitations do you have?

The Mixed Bag of Our Lives and Our Churches

41

COLOSSIANS 4:14–15 NRSV | Luke, the beloved physician, and Demas greet you. Give my greetings to the brothers and sisters in Laodicea, and to Nympha and the church in her house.

Consider This

When I was in seminary (and if you are ever looking for the greatest seminary on the planet, please let me know), I served as the groundskeeper for Rose Hill, the residence of the seminary president, who at the time was Maxie Dunnam. He became a mentor to me in those days and remains so to the present. I remember once, in response to the news that one of our students had committed an unspeakable indiscretion, Maxie lamented to me, "John David, unfortunately, the church is the world."

I've never forgotten it and reflect on it often. On the one hand, the church is the people of God, the saints, or holy ones. At the same time, the church is, as the hymn writer put it, "frail children of dust and feeble as frail."[5] We are those in whom the fullness of God is pleased to dwell, and yet we are prone to fill up our cravings with every emptiness under the sun. We are "in Christ," anchored in heaven, and "in Colossae," with roots yet attached in the soil of sin. The church is the world, and it will only ever be finally sorted out at the end of all things broken and the beginning of all things made new. Our main task is to ask the Lord of the harvest to sort the mixed bag of our own lives now.

That's the story of today's text. On the one hand, Paul salutes Dr. Luke, who would go on to write the gospel bearing his name, and if that weren't enough, the Acts of the Apostles. On the other hand, he lifts up Demas, about whom he will later write to Timothy, "Do your best to come to me quickly, for Demas, because he loved this world, has deserted me and has gone to Thessalonica" (2 Tim. 4:9–10).

In similar fashion, Paul hails the brothers and sisters in Laodicea, to whom the apostle John will later personalize this stinging revelation: "I know your works; you are neither cold nor hot. I wish that you were either cold or hot. So, because you are lukewarm, and neither cold nor hot, I am about to spit you out of my mouth" (Rev. 3:15–16 NRSV).

It's conjecture on my part, but I wonder if that's why Paul gave the hat tip to Nympha. Why would there be another church in Laodicea and this one led by a woman?

Hear John a verse further on them: "For you say, 'I am rich, I have prospered, and I need nothing.' You do not realize

---

5   Robert Grant, "O Worship the King" (public domain).

that you are wretched, pitiable, poor, blind, and naked"
(Rev. 3:17 NRSV).

It seems Nympha may have played host to a splinter
community who could perhaps no longer abide the fruit-
less charades of "First Church." This would have likely made
Nympha a term of derision among the religious elite. Paul
could have scorned this as schismatic or simply said nothing,
but he chose instead to establish her for history and eternity
as a church-planting woman of valor.

The church is the world. It's a confusing place. The wheat
and the tares so often hopelessly intertwined—Demas and
Luke; lukewarm Laodiceans and Nympha's band.

For now we must live in the mess of it all. It's why we will
call Domino #4|14 Our Conundrum. As someone once said,
"The church is like Noah's ark. Had it not been for the flood-
waters outside, who could have stood the stench inside?!"

We must keep coming back to Dominoes #3|9 and #3|10:
"Do not lie to each other, since you have taken off your old
self with its practices and have put on the new self, which
is being renewed in knowledge in the image of its creator"
(Col. 3:9–10).

At the end of the day, our most valuable prayer must mirror
the one we pray at the beginning of the day, "Lord Jesus
Christ, Son of God, have mercy on me a sinner."

The Prayer

Abba Father, we thank you for your Son, Jesus, who will
one day sort the wheat from the tares and establish your

kingdom finally and forever. Grace me to be filled with both compassion and conviction, and by your Spirit form them in the shape of courage to stand as your church in the midst of the world. We pray in Jesus' name. Amen.

The Questions

- If Demas is at one end of the discipleship spectrum and Luke at the other (1–10), where do you locate the state of your own discipleship?
- If First Church Laodicea is at one end of the church spectrum and Nympha's church at the other (1–10), where do you locate the state of your local church?
- How are you dealing with the frustrating reality that the church is the world? *By remembering the sacrifise of Christ, by remembering who we are called to be and reflect.*

42 Why Letters Matter

COLOSSIANS 4:16 | After this letter has been read to you, see that it is also read in the church of the Laodiceans and that you in turn read the letter from Laodicea.

Consider This

Wait! Did he just reference an epistle to Laodicea? Is that in your Bible? It's not in mine. Is it part of the Gospel of Thomas collection or some other apocryphal mystery?

This is the stuff of Da Vinci codes and spy novels—the long-lost letter from Laodicea. Did it contain a secret map disclosing the location of the coveted Holy Grail? Might Ovaltine's Little Orphan Annie secret decoder ring help us interpret some encrypted message should the letter surface today? Nothing like a missing letter from the apostle Paul to stir up biblical intrigue and endless conspiracy theories.

Truth be told, most biblical scholars believe this missing letter to the Laodiceans is actually Paul's letter to the Ephesians, which he intended as a circular letter to make the rounds among all of his churches. He wanted the Colossians to make sure to get a copy of the letter to the Ephesians, which was making its way to them by way of the Laodiceans. How 'bout them apples?! Letters matter . . . a lot.

All kidding aside, is this not exactly what we are doing with the Daily Text? We are circulating Scripture. It seems absurd to even say it, but without parallel or rival, the single most important element of the Daily Text, day in and day out, is the daily text itself—by which I mean the biblical text. The entire goal of the project is to circulate the Word of God and to cause people to engage it, interact around it, and do it. Sure, I add some color and contemporary reflection, but without *the* daily text of Scripture, I have nothing to say.

I wanted to be a writer when I was thirty. I wanted to be a writer like this when I was forty. But let's be honest. At thirty and forty I wanted to be famous. At fifty, I couldn't care less. I want to be faithful. Faithful feels to me like trading on whatever it is God has given me for the advance of his purposes in the world. He has given me his Word and the training to explore its meaning. He has given me half a century of life experience. And he has given me you.

Far from a crowd of passive religious consumers, you are a community of sowers for awakening. You are already banding together in hundreds of counties across this nation alone. We are sowing for a great awakening! And what do we have to sow other than the holy Word of God, taking root in our lives through the power of the Spirit of God in the glorious way of the Son of God, our Lord, Jesus Christ.

This is why we want the Daily Text to spread. It's for the awakening. You are already sowing, sharing it with friends and family. There are about ten thousand of us that we know of. Let's ask God to make us a hundred thousand by this time next year. It's why we are putting the Daily Text into books, so you can sow it into Sunday school classes and small groups and even sermon series for whole churches. (And for the record, I get no royalties from any of this. Everything we get goes right back into sowing for awakening, which is why I want you to buy ten of each!)

> After this letter has been read to you, see that it is also read in the church of the Laodiceans and that you in turn read the letter from Laodicea. (v. 16)

See what I just did there? Now that you are almost through the letter, I want you to see that it is also read by your friends and family, your neighbors, your local church, the church down the street and in the next town over. Pass your copy on or get an extra from Seedbed.com.

The Prayer

Abba Father, we thank you for your Son, Jesus, who is the Word of God. Would you write his life like a letter on our hearts? Would you make his mind our minds? Root out all of the resistance in me. I want to follow Jesus. We pray in Jesus' name. Amen.

The Questions

- Can you start naming one—or three—of the big epiphanies in your life from this journey through Colossians?
- Reflect on Paul's strategy of letter writing and circulation and try to wrap your mind around just how successful the campaign has been and continues to be.
- How have you shared the Daily Text with others in the past?

Why It's Time for You to Enter the Ministry | 43

COLOSSIANS 4:17 | Tell Archippus: "See to it that you complete the ministry you have received in the Lord."

Consider This

I wonder if Archippus was there when they read the letter. Was he on the proverbial fence as to whether he would fulfill his calling? Was he waiting on a word from the Lord? A lot of people are.

Here are the details on Archippus. We have it on good evidence he was a preacher in Colossae. There's pretty good evidence he went on to be the bishop of Laodicea. He is also referenced as a "fellow soldier" in Paul's letter to Philemon (v. 2 NRSV).

So beyond that, what do we do with a verse like, "Tell Archippus: 'See to it that you complete the ministry you have received in the Lord'" (Col. 4:17)?

I've got an idea. Try this.

> Tell [insert your name here]: "See to it that you complete the ministry you have received in the Lord."

You have one, you know—a ministry. In the original Greek language, the word for ministry means "to wait tables." Think about the last time you were at a restaurant where a waiter or waitress served you. In the biblical sense of the term, that server was ministering to you. Where in your life do you find yourself waiting tables as it relates to serving other people?

We are coming to the close of a period of church history where the general understanding has been that one had to be a minister (read, clergy) to have a ministry. Clergy did the "ministry," and the laity helped out around the edges where needed. This model still prevails in a lot of places, but it does not resemble the church envisioned by the New Testament.

You have a ministry. Maybe you've not understood it as such. Maybe you've thought of it as just doing good or doing the right thing or as a civic duty. What if it could be raised to the level of Jesus? What if that ordinary act of service, of waiting tables, could be charged with the energy of the Holy Spirit? The task would still be ordinary, but your touch would carry transformational power through doing it.

Maybe you have a ministry at the local assisted living center. Maybe your ministry is in your work as a lawyer or a doctor or a checker at Wal-Mart. Maybe your ministry is as a crossing guard at an elementary school. Maybe you have a ministry of being Santa Claus during the Christmas season. Perhaps your ministry is driving elderly people to the doctor who can't drive themselves.

Whatever it might be, what would it mean to raise it to the level of Jesus? It would mean at least two things. First, it would mean lowering your stature in the sense of your willingness to take on lower and lower tasks. Second, it would mean raising the level of spiritual power in your service. You are responsible for the first step. Jesus will take care of the second. We see this marvelously at play when Jesus washed his disciples' feet.

"See to it that you complete the ministry you have received in the Lord" (v. 17). It's probably a good word we want to start speaking to each other too.

J. D. WALT

The Prayer

Abba Father, we thank you for your Son, Jesus, who came not to be served but to serve. Give me fresh eyes to see the possibilities to minister to others "in the Lord." We pray in Jesus' name. Amen.

The Questions

- Have you ever thought of yourself as a minister? Why or why not? *Yes, teaching Sunday school*
- What is your ministry? How do you wait on tables?
- What might it look like for your ministry to be raised to the level of Jesus—to go lower in stature and higher in power?

44 The Highlight Reel

COLOSSIANS 4:18 | I, Paul, write this greeting in my own hand. Remember my chains. Grace be with you.

Consider This

And so it ends. Colossians is in the books. Before we leave it behind, I wanted to revisit a few of my favorite highlights. Let's tip these dominoes one more time.

> Paul, an apostle of Christ Jesus by the will of God, and Timothy our brother, To the saints and faithful brothers and sisters in Christ in Colossae: Grace to you and peace from God our Father. (Col. 1:1–2 NRSV)

The issue is not whether we will live in Colossae or not. We must live there or Cincinnati or Centerville or wherever it is we have been appointed to live. The question is whether we will live in Christ or not. Will I become a bona fide in-Christ-one? This is the awakening we must have. This begins to happen when my attention turns from my disgruntlement with the insanity around me to my discontent with the incongruity within me. When this awakening becomes greater and greater within us, it leads to the awakening becoming greater and greater around us.

> In our prayers for you we always thank God, the Father of our Lord Jesus Christ, for we have heard of your faith in Christ Jesus and of the love that you have for all the saints, because of the hope laid up for you in heaven. You have heard of this hope before in the word of the truth, the gospel that has come to you. Just as it is bearing fruit and growing in the whole world, so it has been bearing fruit among yourselves from the day you heard it and truly comprehended the grace of God. (Col. 1:3–6 NRSV)

To be sure, the gospel is the message of what God has done for us in Jesus Christ, but in a far greater sense, the gospel is who Jesus Christ is to us and in us and through us for the world. The gospel is not a body of knowledge about who God is and what God has done. It is actually *knowing* God.

> May you be made strong with all the strength that comes from his glorious power, and may you be

> prepared to endure everything with patience, while joyfully giving thanks to the Father, who has enabled you to share in the inheritance of the saints in the light. He has rescued us from the power of darkness and transferred us into the kingdom of his beloved Son, in whom we have redemption, the forgiveness of sins. (Col. 1:11–14 NRSV)

I think I used to think I didn't need to be rescued, that I wasn't one of those kinds of people. Sure, I knew I was a sinner, but not that bad. I just needed a little Sunday school–esque straightening of the collar. Now I know better. The kind of sinner I thought I was is actually the worst kind of sinner because we think since we didn't ride the *Titanic* to the bottom of the ocean, we somehow don't need as much grace as the ones who did. Now I recognize this as a lie from the pit of hell. The dominion of darkness is oh-so-deceptive. We all must be rescued, especially me. In fact, I will never become a real Christian until I know I am a real sinner.

> The Son is the image of the invisible God, the firstborn over all creation. For in him all things were created: things in heaven and on earth, visible and invisible, whether thrones or powers or rulers or authorities; all things have been created through him and for him. (Col. 1:15–16)

We must see Jesus. We were made to behold him. His life, not in general but in a thousand specifics, must become our vision. His preexistence, preeminence, conception, birth, life, words, deeds, miracles, relationships, signs, sermons, parables, prayers, suffering, passion, death, burial, resurrection, ascension, return, and eternal reign must become our holy obsession. This is the message Paul offers the Colossians and the Colombians, the Americans and the Africans, and everyone else. We must see Jesus. We must fix our gaze upon him.

> I want you to know how hard I am contending for you and for those at Laodicea, and for all who have not met me personally. My goal is that they may be encouraged in heart and united in love, so that they may have the full riches of complete understanding, in order that they may know the mystery of God, namely, Christ, in whom are hidden all the treasures of wisdom and knowledge. (Col. 2:1–3)

The way is together. Here's the part that is not apparent to those of us who happen to be twenty-first-century Americans. When Paul identifies the mystery as "Christ in you," what he really means is "Christ in y'all." The *you*, as is the case so often in the New Testament, is plural. The New Testament rarely addresses me as an isolated, individuated, privatized person. To be sure, God addresses me personally, but my identity is not primarily as an individual. In fact, this is more a sign of my brokenness. I simply cannot know who I am outside of my relationship with God. And here's the kicker: I can't know God apart from other people. That's where we want to push back.

> Put to death, therefore, whatever belongs to your earthly nature: sexual immorality, impurity, lust, evil desires and greed, which is idolatry. (Col. 3:5)

What would it mean to walk that last mile, escorting my sins to the death chamber? How many times have you walked your sins to the death chamber only to walk them back to the cell again?

> Therefore, as God's chosen people, holy and dearly loved, clothe yourselves with compassion, kindness, humility, gentleness and patience. (Col 3:12)

Compassion, kindness, humility, gentleness, and patience aren't virtues to which we must aspire. No, they are our uniform. Think of them as the pads a football player wears to play the game. Mustn't this be what Paul means when he says "clothe yourselves"?

The dominoes keep on tipping. May they never stop.

The Prayer

Abba Father, we thank you for your Son, Jesus, who is the Word behind every word of your Word. Make me a person of this Word, all the days of my life. We pray in Jesus' name. Amen.

The Questions

- What insight(s) do you take away from this journey through Colossians?
- What are the implications of this insight?
- What intention(s) do you carry forward?